The

PRAYERS

of
Father
Killian

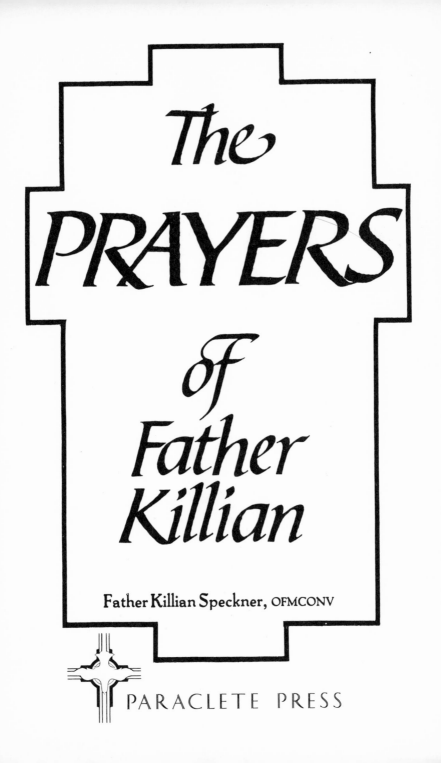

The
PRAYERS
of
Father
Killian

Father Killian Speckner, OFMCONV

PARACLETE PRESS

Acknowledgements

I thank all of the Franciscan Sisters of Mishawaka, Indiana for their kindness during the time I spent there.

I thank Sister Geraldine Hartke who was encouraging and instrumental in getting this book published.

I thank Teresa Wedler for typing the manuscript so many times.

I thank David Manuel for his kindness, appreciation and encouragement.

Dedicated
To My Sister,
Sr. Rose Speckner, O.P.
who loved others
into new life.

Foreword

Originally, this collection of vesper prayers was not intended for publication. It grew through two years of ministering as chaplain to the Franciscan Sisters of Mishawaka, Indiana. I had the opportunity to share with them some of the thoughts that came to me from the readings of Scriptures and the celebrations of Feast days.

It is now offered with the invitation to use the prayers however they will be most beneficial: private moments of need to pray, introductions to meditation, at the end of a period of prayer, or in conjunction with the suggested reading. As you can see, there is one for each day of the year. Generally, the prayers correspond to the liturgical season of the year, but the suggested readings are not necessarily those of the day. It is hoped that by fixing a date for Lent and Easter, it will not be too confusing.

These daily prayers reflect the agonies, struggles, failures, joys and hopes of the human spirit — the story of most of us who live uneasily at times in the presence of God, who do what we don't want to do, and don't always do what we should do. I hope that each prayer will be a comfort, an inspiration and a blessing for everyone who prays.

—*Fr. Killian Speckner,* OFMCONV

We kneel in the midst of the scene of Bethlehem once again. We can only marvel at what has happened here.

This little one, this infant, wrapped warmly and held so tenderly, is not only the Son of Mary, but the Son of God Himself.

This mother, whose face is lighted by a small fire, whose face is shining from the fire within, is the Mother of God. It is frightening to be here, but the angel said not to be afraid. This Jesus has come into the world for our salvation, so we can be temples of God, so we can also be filled with our Lord and give birth to Him through the way we live and are.

Rid us, Lord, of all sin and let us be filled with Your light and fire.

Luke 2:16-21

January 2

J esus, help us to continue to prepare a place
for You in the whole geography of our lives;
there are hills and valleys that need to be made
straight; there are closets of darkness that need
to be lighted.

Jesus, we can't be satisfied with having You
in only part of our lives; we need You to fill us
in everything we do, in every place we live. We
know that it isn't enough for us to be with You
in church, at prayer time, but we must live
with You and through You, all day and all
night.

Thank You for this season of the year, for
reminding us of Your total love for us.

John 1:19-28

January 3

Father in heaven, we thank You again and again for giving us Your Son, for sending Him into the world, to show us how much You love us. We sometimes forget to be grateful; we sometimes seem to love ourselves more than we love You.

Forgive us our weaknesses, heal our sinfulness, give us an awareness of the presence of Jesus in the world and in our lives. Let us understand and teach others how holy the world is for having had Jesus live here. Let us reverence all things, since all things were created through Your Word. Let us treat one another as holy, since You treasure everyone as Your own. Help us to live as Jesus lived.

Matthew 1:18-23

January 4

Jesus, we thank You for the invitation to "Come and see" where You live. It is the only way we are going to know who You are, and it is the only way we are going to learn who we are. You call us to come to live with You, to watch You in the way You treat others, to hear what You say in speaking of Your Father's will, in every moment of Your suffering and every moment of your joy. We must come to You within the depths of our own hearts; we need to sit there in silence day after day, until we absorb Your presence and really understand that You are everything in all of us.

Let me give You the praise that only I can give You and that is by trying to be with You and be like You.

John 1:35-42

J esus, You called each of us to follow You, as You call everyone born into this world, to become part of Your Kingdom. It isn't that You call all in general, but You invite everyone individually, because You know everyone intimately; You delight in thinking that every human being is worthy of being loved and is capable of loving, as You desire us to do. Your invitation to us is spoken to us alone, and we have the freedom to say yes or no. Let our approach to every day be a complete yes. Let our response be positive and loving, no matter how we are feeling or what burdens we are carrying.

Thank You for inviting us. Let us begin to follow You.

John 1:43-51

January 6

Jesus, You are given treasures and visited by those men who represent all of the countries of the world, all of the different tribes and cultures, all peoples who have been and are to be. You have called all the world to worship and serve You. When we see so many people who don't know You, so many who do not follow Your gospel of peace and poverty, we have to push away the doubts that come into our hearts. We do believe that somehow You will restore all things and all people to the Father, that You will come again to make all things new.

Help us to help in that promise, by living as You have called us to live, in love of everyone, in detachment from earthly things, in waiting in expectation for Your coming again into the world.

Matthew 2:1-12

January 7

J esus, it is so hard for us to see beyond the burden we bear or past the yoke You gave us. We so often concentrate upon our own feelings, our own pain, and we think that is the most important thing in the world. We don't always realize that the present burden we must carry will make tomorrow's joy all the more welcome. We forget that we have to suffer and bear pains of human life, if we are to grow to maturity in our spiritual life, if we are to become the loving people You want us to be.

Let us willingly take up our cross and follow You, knowing that the reward You promised is greater than our hearts can imagine; the Kingdom You are leading us to is worth the dying day by day.

Matthew 11:25-30

Jesus, how many times have You looked at me with pity; how many times have You seen me going in the wrong direction, searching for my own fulfillment, self-seeking; how much of my life I have been like a sheep without a shepherd. But I think of the story You told of the shepherd who would leave the 99 and go to find the one who was lost. So You love me. So You have invited me again and again to come back to You.

Teach me always to listen for Your voice calling me; help me to long for the security of Your arms around me; lead me every day, in all I do, in the path You want me to follow with You.

Mark 6:34-44

Jesus, there is no reason to be afraid, when I know that You are always near. But fear is often something that we can't control; we don't even understand where it comes from at times. Even when it is impossible to see any light, help me to think of You, saying to Your disciples: "Don't be afraid; it is I." You are more powerful than any evil force; You are more loving than anyone I could ever imagine; You desire my salvation; You forgive my offenses; You want to live in me, and I want to live in You. I want to put my trust entirely into Your hands; You know all things; You know that I love You.

Mark 6:45-53

Jesus, even though we can't sit in church and hear You expound the Scriptures for us, we are twice blessed: we can read all that You said, while You were in this world, and we can sit in Your presence that is within us. Your Spirit dwells in our hearts, so we can say, as You did: "The Spirit of the Lord is upon me."

We want all other things to pass us by; we want nothing of this world to take possession of us; we want only to be aware of and responsive to Your Spirit within us. Continue to come into our hearts, to recreate us, moment by moment, so we will be more truly Yours — more totally one with You.

Luke 4:14-22

Jesus, help me to believe that You will do the curing of all people who suffer from any illness, that You do want to see justice and peace triumphant in the world, that You desire for all the poor to be fed, clothed and cared for. I don't understand how evil can be so all-pervasive in the world, after Your death and resurrection. I don't even understand how any of us can sin after having known You and loved You. I'm not asking for understanding or knowledge; let me believe in You, hope in You and love You with all of my being. I put all of my doubting into Your hands, knowing that some day all my questions will be answered, doubts taken away, and faith justified by the very sight of You.

Luke 5:12-16

Father in heaven, we give You thanks for all the joy in heaven over the return of sinners to the path of virtue. We know ourselves what joy there was in our hearts when we repented and came back to You. And we always rejoice for those we know who have found their way to repentence. We ask You to let us share more in the return of sinners by our fervent prayers, for our acts of penance, by whatever effort we can make in our lives to entice others to love You and to serve You more faithfully. Let us even be willing to lay down our lives for others, if that would be necessary. We offer this prayer in the name of the One through whom we are all brought to salvation, Jesus, our Lord.

Luke 15:3-7

January 13

Father, You are faithful to all who love and
serve You. We witness how Your chosen one,
Abram, was guided by You, over and over, to
fulfill the destiny You desired for him. We
praise You for the good that You gave to our
father Abraham. And we thank and praise
You for the good You have given to us. When
we put all our trust in You; when we leave
everything in Your hands, You find the way for
us to go. You have given us the strength to bear
the Cross; You have lighted our way in the
greatest darkness. Help us always to turn to
You in our doubts, when we have problems,
when we are confused. You alone are our
strength; You alone know where You want to
lead us; Your will alone is our desire. Draw us
to Yourself, as You drew Abram and all those
ancient ones who claimed you as their God.

Genesis 13:2, 5-18

January 14

J esus, we pray for all of the church, that
everyone who has been given the gift of faith in
You will be conscious of the need to call others
to faith. We believe that You are the Way, the
Truth and the Life. We believe that eternal life
is found only through You. We wish with all of
our hearts for all human beings to know You
and believe in You. We pray to the Father, in
Your name, to send laborers into the harvest,
to make all Christians aware of the need to be
more involved in teaching the Gospel, in living
it in faith, that they might attract others to
come to know You. We ask for courage for
ourselves, so we may live the Gospel more
faithfully, so we will give the example that
others need to discover You in themselves.

Mark 1:14-20

January 15

Jesus, when You preached and worked miracles, many people came to believe in You, many followed You and stayed with You. But many more were not impressed; their hearts were closed to You forever. We pray for all those people who for whatever reason have not responded to Your message and have remained indifferent or even hateful toward You. We pray for those who have responded through baptism but have not lived the Gospel life; we pray for ourselves, that we will be more loving and caring for one another, more aware of those in need of You, more concerned that You will be known and loved by all in the world.

Mark 1:21-28

January 16

Jesus, when Barnabas and Saul were sent
out by the Spirit to spread the Word, they went
as an extension of the Twelve You had first
chosen for Yourself. You knew that down
through the centuries, men and women from
every country would be called to preach the
Gospel. There are millions who left all things
to follow You. People who left their homes and
died in foreign lands. And the same thing
happens every day in our own time. Help us,
too, to be part of this group by living faithfully
Your teaching with all of our strength. If we
can rid ourselves of all selfishness, of all
indifference and try to offer You every moment
and deed of our lives, we, too, can be
instruments in leading others to You. Give us
that grace and strength.

Acts 12:24—13:5

Jesus, we thank You for the gift of St Paul in our own lives. For generations, he has instructed believers in the faith. You have made his own faith immortal. You knew that he would be instrumental in the growth of Your church in the world, and especially among the Gentiles. Teach us to understand what the Spirit is telling us, through the writings of St Paul. Let his influence in our lives help us to influence others to love You more and serve You better in faith. Let his example make us open to all You are telling us by the events in our lives and through others. Hear our prayers for the conversion of all sinners.

Acts 9:1-20

H ow happy we are, Jesus, for the paralyzed man and his friends. Their faith certainly was strong to bring him all that way. They refused to give up, when the crowd was too large to get through, and so they carried their sick friend to the roof. They were sure You would heal him. And You gave them all an even greater gift, by telling the paralyzed one that his sins were forgiven. No one had ever done that before. What a joy it was for him! He must have run all the way home, so he could sit and think of that. And how blessed we are to know that You have forgiven us our sins! Over and over. We have been blessed by You. Let us sit and contemplate how You love us; let us treasure the presence of Your Spirit within us.

Mark 2:1-12

Jesus, give us the same spirit of love that You had for the sinners of this world. Sometimes we put ourselves in the class of the self-righteous, and look down upon, even despise, those people who are public sinners, who get their names in the paper or are known to everyone as public sinners. There is no one in the world that we can point a finger at and say we are better. There is no one in the world we can judge. Let our hearts reach out to all people in our prayer and in the sacrifices we make for them. Teach us to love everyone and to tell them so.

Have mercy on us, the greatest of sinners.

John 8:3-11

ather, we thank You for the example of trust and strength that You give us in the lives of Abraham and Isaac, and of all those chosen people of early times. It seems that You truly walked among them; that they heard Your voice and followed Your will, the best they could.

   We thank You especially for Jesus, who lived among us, too, who lives with us and in us at this time, at all times. We ask You to continue to strengthen us and make us open to Your love for us. Teach us day after day to put all of our trust in You. Our lives belong to You; there is no other reason to live, except to do Your will. Help us to do that. Help us to know that You will continue to be with us, and that You will lead us to do Your will in all things.

Genesis 23:1-4

Father, it seems that Jacob and his mother
were cheating when they arranged it that Isaac
gave his fatherly blessing to Jacob instead of to
his eldest son. But as so many things in Your
history among us tell us, we can only believe
that this was done according to Your will; that
You who are the Father of all law and all life
can arrange events in life anyway You want.
We ask You to continue to arrange things in
our lives, that they will be for Your honor and
glory. Some events are completely strange and
not intelligible, but we must trust that You can
bring good out of them. We offer our lives to
You and ask You to make them good, correct
the evil You see there, build up the virtue,
make us willing to accept all things from Your
hands with praise and glory.

Genesis 27:1-5, 15-29

F ather, we thank You for the covenant you made with Jacob and with all of your faithful people. We thank You for the new covenant You have made with us: the gift of the body and blood of Jesus, which we can hold up to You each day, as forgiveness of our sins, as a promise of the eternal life which we long for and hope for. Help us to be always faithful to Your covenant. Especially let us see how important are all the acts of our lives, which we offer to You and dedicate to You. Help us that our words and actions, and our relationships with others, will bring all of us to love You more and give You praise in our daily lives. We are not here in this life to do our own wills but, as Your Son said, to do the will of our Father in heaven. We trust that You will show us each day what You want of us and that You will give us the inspiration and strength to do it.

Genesis 28:10-22

January 23

F ather, we thank You for the example of
Joseph and his brothers that You give us in the
book of Genesis. It is a beautiful story of
forgiveness, and how You provide for those
who love You and are faithful in Your service.
Sometimes we feel that we are abandoned or
that there is only darkness and despair in our
lives, but we know that we have to put
ourselves entirely into Your hands. Even if it
seems that You will allow us to be killed, we
must trust You and know and believe that
Your will is to be done in Your way and in
Your own time.

   We do trust You and put ourselves day after
day entirely into Your hands, so that we might
praise You even when things seem to go the
way we had not planned or expected. We only
ask that Your will be done and not our own.

Genesis 44:18-21

Jesus, the remarkable cures that You worked through the prayers of St Peter make us rejoice even in our day. This man who was afraid on the lake and began to sink, who denied You in the courtyard and ran away in fear, soon changed into the person You had called him to be — one not afraid of anything, one with the greatest faith in Your power and presence. As we praise him, we also pray that our faith might be as strong as his, and that You will use us as You used him: to bring others to You, that You will give us the power to grow in faith, and grow through our many sins and failures.

Acts 9:31-42

January 25

Joseph asked his brothers (who were afraid
that he would kill them), if he could take the
place of God by taking revenge on them.
Father, we ask Your forgiveness for trying to
take your place in so many ways in our lives.
We judge others in our own mind and condemn
them; we invade their lives and think that we
are destined to tell them what You do for them.
We assume that we are great in Your eyes and
that others are less important. How completely
we condemn ourselves when we act that way!
Joseph was blessed by You with great gifts, yet
he was humble and knew that all he had, came
from You. Teach us to be that wise, to know
that we are not meant to take your place in the
lives of others. Teach us to know who we are
and to give all things into Your hands.

Genesis 49:29-33, 50:14-24

January 26

J esus, we thank You for the vocation to
which You have called us. We realize that the
little we do does not have much impact on the
vastness of the harvest that is waiting to hear
Your word. But we also know that we are
merely instruments in Your hands, and You
can accomplish whatever You please through
the work of Your Spirit in us. We ask You only
to let us be willing and responsive instruments.
Let us hold nothing back through laziness or
any lack of enthusiasm. We pray You to use us
in any way You desire. And let us always hear
Your voice calling us, so that we can respond
with all of our being, in whatever way you
would have us.

Luke 10:1-9

January 27

Jesus, we give You thanks for those days in
Antioch, when Barnabas and Paul instructed
so many in the faith. We can imagine the
community growing rapidly and the fervor
which filled the spirits of all those who
responded to Your Spirit. It is a time to
remember when the Spirit was poured out so
generously upon both Jew and Greek. It is a
place to remember where the followers of the
way were called after You, Christians. We bear
that name with pride.

We pray that we may give honor to Your
name in the way we live, so that all who know
us will respond also with reverence to Your
name and to Your teaching. Let Your name be
the way in which we identify ourselves and by
which we know ourselves and the work that we
have to do.

Acts 11:19-26

January 28

J esus, we ask You to let us be always in the
hands of the Father. We know that this world
is full of evil; it threatens us from every side.
But we belong to You, we are called by Your
name, we have pledged ourselves to serve
always under Your banner. We thank You for
keeping us safe from the power of Satan, and
we beg You to break the bondage that Satan
has over so many people in this world. We
believe that in Your name, through the prayers
of all who believe in You, that the power of evil
will be overcome. Give us the grace to
persevere always in this faith and hope. We
offer all of this world to You, so You can keep
us free from Satan's power.

Mark 3:22-30

T hank You, Jesus, for claiming us as Your own. Thank You, for letting us know that all people who believe in You are truly our brothers and sisters. And thank You also, for filling our hearts with Your love, so we can love all of Your family here on earth, even as we love ourselves. We know You especially want us to love those little ones, those who are suffering in any way from any neglect in this world — for these "least" share more in Your suffering and death than all the others. We ask You to forgive us this day, for any lack of love there has been in our lives and especially for any hurt we may have caused any of our brothers and sisters.

Mark 3:31-35

January 30

Jesus, we don't know how long we are to be in this world, but we ask that You protect us from all of the evils that can attack us (from within and without) and cause us not to bear the fruit that You except of us all of our lives. We know and believe that nothing we do is of value because of ourselves, but only because Your grace makes it good. We know and believe that any failure in the work we do is from our own weakness. We pray that You will keep us close to You, so we will persevere in the remaining days, trying always to do Your will, trying always to give You honor and glory by our lives.

Mark 4:1-20

Jesus, You have reminded us many times that we have nothing that has not come from Your love, that has not been given us by You. There is nothing that we have that belongs to us alone. And all You have given us is meant to be given away. Help us give of our love to others, to those who feel they are unloved, to those who are in some need of love. Let us desire with all of our hearts that they grow in grace and love in Your presence. Let us give of our time to those who need someone to help them, to those who need someone to listen. Teach us to understand that all we hold back will become only ashes, but what we give away will come back to us one hundredfold.

Mark 4:21-25

Jesus, it is impossible for us to understand how we came to the faith that You have given us. You chose us; we didn't choose You. Let us help to spread the reign of God by all that we do. The more we express our faith through the love we have for others, through the good that we do in this world, the more we will help to inspire others to strengthen their faith, to find the pearl of the Kingdom, to grow in love of You and their brothers and sisters.

We tremble at the thought of ever losing the faith. We ask You to let us rather die than to give up or lose the faith we have in You.

Mark 4:26-34

February 2

Jesus, we give You thanks for the people in our lives who have pointed the way for us by their word and example. We are thinking especially of older men and women, our grandparents, aunts, uncles, and older religious who drew so close to You during their lives that they seemed to live with You every moment. Give us the grace, too, to be aware of Your nearness to us and to others. Send Your Spirit into our lives, to let us be instruments of grace for others.

We pray that our words and example will be light to those in darkness, comfort for those sorrowing, peace for those disturbed.

Luke 2:22-40

I know I will never understand in this life the mystery of sickness, pain, and the death of those I love. In Your life on earth, Jesus, some are healed — those You don't see, those at a distance, those You touch, those You lift from their death beds. It is natural to ask: Why these? Why not others? Why not your foster father, Joseph? But I won't get an answer. I can only accept the wonderfulness of Your power and Your response of love. But I pray for all those who suffer in the world and all those who die young. I pray that they may have the strength to bear what they have to bear, to recognize Your presence in their suffering. I pray that they will come within Your kingdom of light and be given the fullness of joy.

Mark 5:21-43

February 4

Jesus, I know that, if I put the Father's will ahead of all else in my life, I will (humanly speaking) always do and say what God wills of me. There are many times when I don't know what to say to others. I have to look within my heart and seek Your Spirit, to know what it is You want me to say. Let my words always begin in You, be presented in Your name, and take rest in You in the hearts of others. Teach me to remember how important words are, how I should treasure them, so that they will not do any harm to others, but that every word I speak will give You honor and glory, and cause others to love You more.

Matthew 10:16-25

February 5

Today, Jesus, You told us to be the salt of the earth, the light of the world.
Renew our fervor, our enthusiasm to make the lives of others more joyful. Take from us the armsful of darkness we hang onto.

Let Your light shine in us, let it show in our eyes, let it sparkle in the words we speak to one another.

The reason we kneel before You now
and worship You
is to become like You,
is to hold You in our arms,
is to become one with You.
Make us a joy to be with,
so we won't die with any regrets
for having lived and loved.
Make us salt and light
to renew the world we live in.

Matthew 5:13-16

February 6

Jesus, we do rejoice for the lives and times of
Your martyrs: Paul Miki, and the other
Franciscans and Jesuits. Preaching Your Good
News in a world where evil has great power can
lead some to despair and bring others to their
deaths. We pray You that there will always be
men and women who will be unafraid to preach
and live the Gospel life. We pray that we
ourselves will never tire of living out the
Gospel, so that others may also be influenced
to live according to Your way. We don't ask
that we will see the good results of our lives, but
only that we will always do all we do for Your
honor and glory and the salvation of souls.

Matthew 16:24-27

February 7

Jesus, we know that some people are more contemplative than others, but all of us have an inner self where we can be alone with You, whenever we give You the time. We ask that You keep reminding us, as You reminded Martha, that choosing to be with You is the better thing, the only thing. We can be with You, as we go about our work, but then we should reflect Your presence when others interrupt us, or the work becomes frustrating. Teach us that Your presence is an inexhaustible treasure; we can find there everything we need for any day, any moment of our lives. Let us remember we are with You always.

Luke 10:38-42

J esus, every day we can worship You in the Sacrifice of the Mass; we invite You into our lives in the Sacrament of the Eucharist; we adore You in the most holy Sacrament of the altar.

Sometimes we are completely distracted at those moments, sometimes we may even be indifferent, sometimes we are far from understanding what we are doing. But we truly don't desire to honor You only with our lips and not with our hearts. We don't want to be hypocrites. We would like to be different; we would like our hearts to be flames of love. Create in us new hearts — like the Immaculate Heart of Mary, and the loving hearts of Your saints. We praise You and honor You in the hearts of all those who love You with more fervor than we find in ourselves.

Mark 7:1-13

February 9

Jesus, You once told Your disciples to go apart to a lonely place to rest. You tell us that, too. There are times when we must isolate ourselves from our business, our busy-ness, noise, all disturbance.

There are times when we need a lonely place, where You can heal us and renew us.

We ask You to give us the grace to respond to that call from You. Give us the courage and humility to admit that we need to rest now and then, to pause and re-collect ourselves. We thank You for this invitation and for the grace to accept it.

Mark 5:30-34

Jesus we know that the death of John the
Baptizer must have brought great pain to Your
heart. His whole life was preparing for You.
He always lived on the edge of pain and death.
He wandered in the desert and fed on whatever
he could find; he was a threat to all who
listened to him, when he reminded them that
they had to change their lives or face the wrath
of God. And the evil he fought against, caught
and put him in the prison cell and to death.

Jesus, let us remember John and be truthful
and honest in what we say and do.

Mark 6:14-29

W hen we were baptized, the priest touched our ears and mouth and said: "The Lord Jesus made the deaf hear and the dumb speak. May He soon touch your ears to receive His Word, and your mouth to proclaim His faith, to the praise and glory of God the Father."

Jesus, we ask You to touch us each day, that we will hear the mystery of Your Word, that it will enter our hearts and bear fruit. Each time we hear it, You reveal something new to us, for Your Word is a living word that will never grow old. Let Your Word be on our lips, that we may grace those we speak to and speak with. Your Word is our strength, our joy, our salvation.

And You are the Word made flesh.

Be with us each day of our lives.

Mark 7:31-37

ather, we have said "Yes" to You, through Your Son, Jesus Christ, over and over in our lives. But sometimes we have said "no," thinking: it slipped out. And at other times, we have said "no" deliberately. We know You understand our weakness and forgive us.

Our hearts want to say "Yes" all the time. But we need Your power in us to do that. Come to us now, again, this day, with Your Holy Spirit, and let us say "Yes" forever. Let our commitment to You be real, thorough, and forever. Focus our eyes on You, direct our hearts to You; take our lives in Your hands and hold us close, so that always and everywhere we will live out our "Yes."

Matthew 5:17-37

Jesus, of all the cures You worked for those around You, that of healing the blind seems somehow to be the most beautiful. We know what the gift of sight is for us; how terrible it would be not to have it. So it makes our hearts rejoice more when we read of Your healing the blind.

Sometimes, our hearts are blind, in not seeing what You want us to see. Sometimes, we look at our brothers and sisters and don't really see them, don't understand their needs. Heal us of any blindness You find in us. Give us the sight that comes with wisdom, compassion, understanding, and love.

Mark 8:22-26

February 14

S t Valentine seems to have been put in the
closet, as far as the liturgy goes. All those strange
and sentimental myths about him, however,
won't be forgotten. And the lacy cards with
flying cherubs and throbbing hearts will always
be with us.

The good of Valentine's Day is the
remembrance of friends. So many people, so
many different types of people have been and are
good to us, and many love us. We are grateful to
God for these gifts. We are thankful that there
are so many people to love — and not only those
who love us. We pray that our love for others will
continue to grow to be more and more, and draw
all of us more surely into that center of love who
is God.

John 14:1-4

When I think of You, Jesus of Nazareth, completely human, a person like me in all things except sin, and, at the same time, *the Christ*, Son of God, it almost makes my breath stop. You became hungry, thirsty, tired; You got rained on; You suffered and died — because You, God, loved me unconditionally and do now and will forever. What can I give to You for loving me? I can't give You anything less than my total self. All my love, all those I love, all I can possibly give, until I have nothing more to give.

Teach me to love Your love.

Mark 8:27-33

Jesus, some of the words we say about following You and loving You are very high and mighty. They are so easy to say, but they are very difficult to mean. Maybe someday I'll wake up and find that I haven't followed You at all; that I've only done my own thing.

Let me say it all again: I will follow You, wherever You will lead me. But You know it is all up to You. I want to. But unless You draw me; unless You give the strength, unless You compel me by Your love, I can't make it. Thank You, Jesus, for accepting me among Your followers.

Mark 8:34—9:1

Jesus, so many times in our lives You show Yourself to us — we are as certain as we can be of who You are, how You love us, and how we love You.

But there are dark times, too — times when we don't think of You with any depth, for weeks or months, when we don't feel Your presence, when we don't feel any love for You. There are times of doubt, when we think: what if those who don't believe, are right? At this moment, in the presence of the Sacrament of Your body and blood, we just want to ask You again: Please keep showing Yourself to us, or we will die of missing You.

Mark 9:2-13

February 18

Jesus, my prayer today is to ask You to teach
and help me love those who bother me with the
petty things they say and do. I know it is pride
that makes me irritated with those who don't
think and feel as I do. I want to be able to seek
them out, to listen to them, to do any service for
them that would please them. Even if it takes the
rest of my life, help me love those who don't love
me, who get on my nerves, who are hard to get
along with. It is the only way I can show You
that I love You.

    Help me to work at it day by day.

      Give me an increase of love,

         so I can share it with those around me.

Matthew 5:33-48

February 19

S t Francis said, "Many a person who may
seem to us a child of the devil, will one day be a
disciple of Christ." In the Gospel of Mark
(9:14-29) the disciples failed to cast a devil out of
the epileptic boy. Jesus said they were faithless.
Sometimes we can't help others or direct them to
Jesus, because we haven't broken completely
the devil's hold in our lives. Some small ways the
devil holds us: through our angers, our
contempt for others, our feeling of superiority;
putting our own wills, our desires, before all
else, even before the will of God.

Jesus, break any hold Satan may have on us.
Let us be empty as Francis was,
empty of our own wills and filled with
only You, only Your love.

Mark 9:14-29

February 20

Jesus, we know that we belong to You. And that includes everything we have and do and are. I awake in the morning, knowing that I awake in Your presence; You take me by the hand and lead me through the day. No matter what activities I engage in, I do them with you. Whatever thoughts I have I share them with you; whatever feelings and emotions come to me, I know that You are involved in them, too.

Because I belong to You, I want to share everything with You — my delight in the beautiful things I see, in the people I meet and talk to of love during the day, in my joy at just being alive.

And when I end the day and retire to sleep, I will say Your name, so Your love is near. Jesus, I belong to You.

Mark 9:41-50

February 21

At the end of the day, we look back at the path
which we have walked. We touch again the
words and actions that have sprung from our
hearts. Forgive us, if we have frowned instead of
smiling. Forgive our turning away, rather than
embracing. Forgive us for judging instead of
being compassionate. Forgive us for shouting
rather than laughing. Forgive us for being
mean.

Today is almost gone; tomorrow is another
beginning. We shall awake with a new heart.
We shall try to love You more; we shall love
ourselves, and with those two gifts we shall show
our love for others just as they are, not trying to
change them. Loving them as You love them —
as You love us.

Mark 7:14-23

February 22

S t Peter was one whose heart was given
completely to Jesus, his master, from the very
beginning. Though they were different, they
had a lot in common. They said what they
thought; they had the courage to die for what
they knew to be right. They had a vision which
extended to the whole world. That spirit of Jesus
and Peter has been handed down to us through
the Church of Christ. It is our faith. We are,
heart and soul, part of that tradition.

We pray for the honesty to be ourselves
completely before all others; for the courage to
live by the law of love, for the commitment to
dedicate our lives to fostering that faith in the
lives of others.

We thank God for the example He has given
us in the life of St Peter, the first Apostle.

Matthew 16:13-19

February 23

Jesus, we see Your signs all around us. Since we love the spirit of St Francis, we appreciate everything that reminds us of You: all the beautiful things of nature that have Your name written on them. We recognize Your presence — Your sign — in the lives of our brothers and sisters. They, too, are dedicated to You; they are a sign of Your presence.

We would like to embrace all things living and beautiful, for they are memories of You. We treasure them, we respect them, we offer them back to You as the gifts You have given us. Thank You, Jesus of Nazareth, for being to us the sign of the Father's love.

Mark 8:11-13

February 24

F ather, we thank You for the love You have
created into the the world — in the love that a
man has for a woman, and woman for a man. We
thank You for the love our parents had for one
another, for our own lives which are the fruit of
that love. We ask You to continue to bless with
the presence of Your Holy Spirit, all human
love. Heal the hurts with which lovers injure one
another. Bind the hearts of those in love together
in Your own bosom. Teach us not to be afraid of
showing love for others. Though You haven't
called all to married love, You have commanded
us to love others, as we love ourselves.
Love is never secret;
it must be shown to others and expressed.
Teach us how to love others expressively with
the love You have shared with us in Jesus
Christ.

Mark 10:1-12

February 25

A poet tells us, Lord, that children come from heaven, "trailing clouds of glory." They seem to have a memory of the loving touch of Your creation. They sometimes smile and laugh in that memory. As they grow, they still have the innocence and openness that we envy but want to imitate. Jesus, You loved children. You wanted them to come to You, to climb on Your lap, to hug You. Renew over and over again, our own innocence and child-likeness. Let us put away all false attitudes and the reluctance to be joyful and carefree. To the child-like heart, all things are innocent and pure. Let us rejoice in our own openness, so we will be welcome to climb in Your lap and hug You and hold on to You.

Mark 10:13-16

February 26

Jesus, I know there is a difference between worrying and planning. I have to make plans for tomorrow, for next month or next year. But as You tell me, I don't have to be anxious and worry about it. It is all in Your hands. Plans may be changed or fall apart, and I will try not to get upset, because You are in charge of my life, of all things. I want to leave every moment, every breath, every plan in Your hands.

Let me praise You and thank You at this moment, for the love and care You have for everyone and everything in this world. May You be loved, and praised, and thanked forever and ever.

Matthew 6:24-34

February 27

Jesus, You challenge me every day. You look at me, as You looked at the rich young man, and You love me, and You say that I should let go again of everything that distracts me from You, that keeps me from You. At that moment, when I came to follow You, I was sure I had given up everything. But I continue to accumulate all kinds of things, to hold onto them, and make them part of my life.

Let me begin again today: whatever is keeping me from being totally Yours, I release; take it from me. I want at this moment to be empty. Fill me up with Your love, with Your presence.

All else, I leave in Your hands.

Mark 10:17-27

February 28

Often there are times in our lives — days and weeks, even — when we get down, discouraged, or else things begin to seem dull and routine and boring. There isn't any joy in life, in work, in the community I live in. Then, I turn to You Lord, and ask: "What is wrong with me?" I think that maybe I've lost something; maybe God has forgotten me.

When I get in those moods, I should remember Your promises to those who give up all things to follow You. That is where I want you to focus my eyes and my heart. On that goal. On the eternal life You have promised. On You, who wait for me in a glory I can't imagine. I thank You, for giving me that promise and that hope. Between here and there the road is difficult and often dull. But Your promise renews my joy. Thank You, God, for all Your gifts.

Mark 10:28-31

Jesus, everything You did was for others. You put aside Your glory as the Son of God, You lived in poverty, You died in pain. You became our servant; You washed our feet.

Jesus, let me never think I am more important than You. Let me be what I'm supposed to be: Your servant and the servant of others. There is nothing too lowly, too insignificant, too unnoticed, that I won't be glad to do, in union with You and for others. Teach me day by day, moment by moment, to be emptied of any pride in my own life and to be united with You, the humble, crucified Christ.

Mark 10:32-45

March 1

Let me see again, Jesus. Let me see through the veil that keeps You from my sight. As I look at the Eucharist, let me see Your face looking back at me. Let me see the love in Your eyes, speaking to me. Let me see that face in the face of everyone I look at. Let me see You in my own pains, frustrations, confusion and weariness. Let me see You within my own heart.

Thank You, Jesus, for healing my sight. I want never to be in the darkness again. I long for the day when my sight will be blinded by the brightness of Your glory and my whole being will be absorbed in Your face.

Mark 10:46-52

March 2

I have met people, Jesus, who have no faith in
You, or the Father. Their hearts and minds
were completely closed to knowing You. But
they were good people; they just couldn't
understand or believe.

I realized then, what a great gift You have
given me in my faith. I want to thank You for it, I
thank my parents who took me to be baptized, I
thank my teachers of all kinds who helped that
faith grow. I am grateful for all the
circumstances of my life which helped my faith. I
offer this gift to You now. I hope You are pleased
with it. I hope it will always give You honor and
glory.

Mark 11:11-26

Father, even though you have shown us many signs in the Old Testament; they are not always easy for us to understand. You have performed many works in the history of the world, and we don't know why or what they all mean. Let us realize how lacking in knowledge and understanding we are. Sometimes we assume that we know You and know Your ways, but even though You have created us in Your image, we are not like You. We don't know You. And because we will never know Your ways, we place ourselves completely in Your hands and ask You to do with us as You will. Whatever happens to us, over which we have no control, we will say: this must be from our God. We accept all things from Your hands, trusting that You love us so much that You will keep us from any harm that would take us away from You. Deepen our faith and keep us in the palm of Your hand.

Genesis 16:1-12

March 4

L ord, the only foundation that my life can be built upon and rest upon is to do Your will. What You want is the fullest expression of Your love for me. My own will is often confused. I want some reward now. I want some success, some pleasure, something for myself. I want to do it my way, which isn't always Your way.

Teach me to hunger and thirst to do Your will. I hope to begin my day with that intention: to hear Your voice, to feel Your Spirit direct me to do everything, say everything, think and desire everything that will be most pleasing to You.

Accept the gift of myself
    and do with me whatever You will.

Matthew 7:21-27

March 5

Jesus, You are still suffering and being killed through all of these centuries since Your life on earth. You are dying of hunger and thirst everywhere we look and chiefly because of the greed of others. You are being shot, tortured, imprisoned, by power-hungry governments, by political policies of the ignorant. You are dying in the poor and the innocent.

Help me to identify with my brothers and sisters who are suffering in Your name. Let my prayer reach them and comfort them. Let my sacrifices in union with You have some meaning to change the state of things. Let my love for those I live with help build up the strength of the love that is needed in our world.

Jesus, suffering for me,
   use me for the love of others.

Mark 12:1-12

March 6

J esus, we wish to acknowledge You before all
the world, by the things we do and the things we
say. We can see in the lives of others, when they
speak or act, that sometimes their words and
actions are not from You; they are not living in
You or acknowledging Your presence in the
world. Sometimes we are not as ready to see the
same denial in our own lives. Teach us to
recognize what we are meant to be in this life.
When we look at the saints who have gone before
us, we long to imitate them as they imitated
You. Let us never give up that desire. Let us
treasure it, and keep it in our hearts, so that
every day of our lives we will acknowledge You
before the world in all we say and do.

Acts 2:42-47

J esus, as we enter into Lent, one thing we know is that sin is the only evil, it is the greatest evil. It is death. And one thing we remember, Jesus, is that You loved sinners, You wanted to be with them all the time, they were Your friends. The power of Your love is enough to overcome sin. During Lent, let us grow in love for You and others, so that sin will be diminished in us. We want to love and pray for, and sacrifice for, all sinners in the world, that Your love may enter their hearts. We don't intend to be sad during Lent; we are not going to wear a "holier-than-thou" expression.

Teach us to be joyful from the knowledge and hope that Your love will in the end conquer all sin in the world and conquer us.

Matthew 6:1-6; 16-18

March 8

Jesus, when You died that all creation might be renewed and recreated, You did it because You loved the Father and all others more than You loved Yourself. You never put Yourself first.

There is a monster in us humans, a basic pride that is hard to get rid of. It lifts us up a little above everyone else; it tells us we are better, holier, more faithful to the law; it pushes us out in front of others, so we get attention, and so people will recognize our goodness, our talents, our achievements, our cleverness . . . . It whispers to us, "Look at me. Think of me."

I want to follow You, Jesus, by thinking of others first, by doing for others before I do for myself, by loving others more than I love me. Take my pride from me, so I can follow You in spirit and in truth.

Luke 9:22-25

March 9

Jesus, I can never finish thanking You for the
innumerable times You have healed me
spiritually, for the countless sins You have
forgiven me. Every time I open my mouth, I
want to thank You; every time my heart beats, I
want to thank You; I can never show my
gratitude as I would wish. But let me show it as
best I can, by trying harder not to fail in my love
for You and my love for others. Let Your Spirit
also teach me how unworthy I am, in
comparison with all others who have served You
in this life.

For all these gifts you have given so freely,
I offer You heart-felt and, I hope,
everlasting praise and thanks.

Mark 1:40-45

March 10

I saw a desert in the winter, full of dead things, hungry coyotes, and tumbleweeds blowing. There was nothing that said the name of life.

But spring came and moisture. There was a resurrection — dazzling flowers, exotic plants, running, leaping, crawling life.

Jesus, You are the living water; bring to life my desert heart. Anoint me with Your springtime during Lent. Let me share the flowers of love, leaping laughter, gentle concern with everyone, especially those in need. Let my life be a living stream in the deserts of those You love.

Luke 5:27-32

March 11

F ather, thank You for the gift of life — for the years You have given me to live, for my spirit, mind, and all of my senses. Body and soul, I rejoice in the life You have given to me. I thank You for sharing this life of Your creation in Jesus Christ, for experiencing all of our human emotions, weaknesses, joys and sorrows, everything except sin.

During this season of Lent, I ask You from the bottom of my heart to let me share my life more deeply with others, especially those around me. I want to appreciate them more, to understand where I can be of help to them and act on that, how I can love them more, love them in You, lift them up to You so You will be praised and glorified.

Empty my life of everything that keeps me from loving You. I give You the gift of my life — the gift You gave to me.

Matthew 4:1-11

March 12

W henever I have reached out unselfishly to others, I reached out to You, Jesus. Whenever I have rejected and turned away from others, I turned my back on You, Jesus.

I need to turn my life around in many ways: There are people I ignore and people I take advantage of. There are some to whom I should apologize and admit my faults. There are some I delay in writing, because I don't particularly like them. There are some I have to listen to, because their problems are overwhelming them. There are some I have to comfort and be good to, in spite of the risk.

Be with me, Jesus,
   especially in these days of Lent,
      and let me meet You face to face
         and welcome You in everyone I know
            and meet.

Matthew 25:31-46

March 13

There are some people I have written off,
because they wanted too much of my time, and I
was too lazy to give it. There are some I haven't
forgiven because, they didn't love me as I
wanted them to. There are some who said nasty
things about me, and I just put them out of my
life. So how can I pray to You, my Father, who is
Our Father, and ask Your forgiveness, unless I
forgive all of those on the fringe of my life?

I must reach out to them in some way during
this season of Lent, and ask for their forgiveness;
I must forgive in my heart anyone who has
sinned against me. Then I will be free to love
You as You want me to; then I will be free to love
everyone and expect nothing in return. Forgive
me for these past and present sins of omission
and commission.

Matthew 6:7-15

Jesus, we are surrounded by the signs of Your presence and God's love for us. You have given us the Sacraments which grab hold of us and draw us to You; You have given us Your Word, which feeds us and moves in us; You have given us Yourself in the Eucharist, in Your Holy Spirit. We are surrounded by and filled with Your signs.

And sometimes we seem to be unmoved by all of this attention You pay to us. We can't sit still; we can't be silent. We must proclaim You, announce You, share You with the rest of the world. Make us instruments of Your peace; make us Your arms, Your legs, Your voice so we take the signs You have given us and be signs of Your presence to others.

Luke 11:29-32

March 15

Jesus, increase my faith. I have a hard time with your teaching about asking and receiving. I know I have prayed until my heart was about to break, and I cried for Your help, but I didn't get what I was asking for. Maybe I had the wrong reasons; maybe I was asking for the wrong thing — and looking back at some of those times of long ago, I understand that it must have been better that You didn't give me what I asked. Because everything You intend to give me must be wrapped in Your love for me. And some things I ask for concern just my poor weak human love.

I will keep asking for what I think is good, but if the things I ask for are not expressions of Your love for me, I don't want them.

Jesus, thank You for increasing my faith.

Matthew 7:7-12

March 16

F ather, how blessed we are to have the
advantage of offering You each day the gift of
Your own Son, Jesus. It's a wonder that the fire
of Your love doesn't rush down upon us to burn
us up in our love for You and for one another. If
there is any darkness in our hearts, if there is any
anger, any lack of love, any tension, or
animosity of any kind, burn it up, melt it down,
take it away, so there will be only one love on
Your altar, only one gift — the gift of Jesus Your
Son, and our hearts gathered to Him and to one
another.

How blessed we are to glorify Your Son in the
Eucharist at this moment.
We bless You, we thank You, we praise You.
Make our hearts, one heart, praising You.

Matthew 5:20-26

March 17

M ary, when you stood beneath the Cross, and
Jesus was dying, you heard Him say: "Father,
forgive them, for they don't know what they are
doing." And you forgave them, too: the Roman
soldiers, the scribes and pharisees, the priests,
the mob who didn't know what was going on.
You forgave them and loved them. I pray to
forgive and love all those in the world who don't
know and love Jesus, who don't know and love
others. I pray to love deeply, murderers and
thieves, dictators, politicians, and violent
people.

I offer them all into the hands of Our Father,
may He heal them, and redeem them through
the blood of His Son and your Son, Jesus.

Matthew 5:43-48

March 18

Jesus, Your face has been radiant as the sun in my life this day. It has dissolved the darkness. It has led me through the day, restfully. You are the Beloved Son of the Father. You are my beloved brother.

Let the light of Your face show in my face, so I can see others as You see them — with love, compassion and forgiveness, so I can see their hearts striving to love You and please You in all things. And when I look at these others, let me see Your face, so I can love them as I love You.

Today I thought of the story of Veronica and the soothing cloth with which she touched Your face. I'm sure she could never forget looking into Your eyes.

Let my heart be imprinted with what she saw and the face she touched.

Matthew 17:1-7

S t Joseph was a person of vision and visions.
He heard and listened to Your voice, Father, at
every point of decision in his life. He could see
beyond the present moment, beyond the trials,
difficulties and impossible things he had to do.
He could see the final solution — to do Your will
in all things, to trust, to reach You.

Teach me to look to Joseph, for the example of
his complete trust. Give me the vision to trust
You at this moment, put all of my life and
circumstances into Your hands at this moment.
Give me the vision to trust You with the future,
to see that all time, all events of the world, will
sift down to that centerpoint, in whom and
through whom all things came to be.

I thank You, Lord, for Joseph;
   he gives me courage;
      he gives comfort to the whole church.

Luke 6:36-38

March 20

D aniel Lord, SJ, wrote a book long ago about "humility with a hook." He pointed out that we are often proud of being humble. I know what he means. It's a sweet feeling to know that others see me (at times) as a humble person. I'm very much like the scribes and pharisees You condemned, Jesus.

Teach me to practice humility by being a servant of others. Hold me still, so I don't turn away from people who want my attention in any way. Stop me when I am inclined to make judgments about others, to be critical of them, to tell myself I'm better than others in some ways. I'm forever doing that, and I'm sorry. I want to be like You, Jesus, who humbled Yourself for me, who became a servant for me and all other sinners.

Empty me and let me share in Your humility.

Matthew 23:1-12

Whenever others hurt me, I respond by hurting them if I can, or disliking them and avoiding them. I defend myself in my own mind by thinking how wrong they are, how evil, how lacking in understanding. Will I ever learn, O Lord, to face, accept and forgive all pain and hurt from others as You did? Will You teach me to identify with You, when I am hurt, to bear it with You, to remember that You are bearing it with me, suffering with me? If I am with You always, then I can even love and thank anyone who uses me or hurts me — for then I share in Your passion and Your redemption of the world.

Forgive me, Lord, for my lack of love toward all those I have hurt by my words and actions.

Matthew 20:17-28

L oving Father, every day is a special gift from You. You hand them to us, one by one. How many will there be? One more, five more, a thousand more? We want to teach each day, each moment as a precious gift from You. Treasure it. Use it with love.

We don't have to search for something to do with the time You give us. You provide us with a multitude of people who cross our path, whom we can reach in some way every day, with whom we can share the time and love You give us. You provide us with moments when You seem particularly near, and we can enjoy passing time with You. You provide us with crosses to bear, a yoke that is sweet.

We trust You, Lord, for You are near with Your love for us, You are in each moment of our day, each day of our life.
    We offer all our life to You
        and every day, every moment that remains
        of it.

Luke 16:19-31

March 23

There are thousands of innocent people killed
by others every day throughout the world. It is
overwhelming to think of the hatred that exists
between people, between brothers and sisters,
parents and children. Hatred is a giant shadow,
a hurting darkness that is everywhere, that we
can even reach out and touch. We should weep
forever, for having hurt anyone in any way. For
whatever we did to others, we did to You, Jesus,
Lord, our Redeemer. We shouted at You, we
talked about You, we put obstacles in Your
way, we even hit You. We treated You as badly
as those who put You to death treated You. All
because we didn't love others, as You love us.

Forgive us and change us. Let us make a
special effort every day to be loving and good
toward those we have treated badly.

Matthew 21:33-43, 45-46

March 24

At the Annunciation, the angel told Mary not to be afraid. The vision was overwhelming; the message she heard was more than could be understood. She said: "Let it be done to me."

Jesus, sometimes I'm afraid, when I think of Your coming to live in me. It is more than I can understand. Faith tells me that God lives in me, His Temple. My mind, my spirit, is not big enough, never will be big enough, the whole world isn't big enough to hold the idea of You. But the little portion of existence that is me, You fill up with Your presence. I'm only a small vessel, but I'm full. Let me understand that, let me appreciate that, let me think about it. And when I'm afraid that You aren't there, or that You are too much there, let me pray with Mary: Let it be done, whatever You want.

P. S. Thank You.

Luke 1:26-38

Jesus, I know that I must pray every day for an increase of faith. There will never come a time when I can say: "Enough." Today, I heard again the story of the woman at the well. How thirsty she was! How You filled her (a traditional enemy of Your people) with faith, and changed her life!

Change my life daily with an increase of faith. Grow stronger in me, more overwhelming. Let me thirst more and more for Your Word, for Your presence in the Blessed Sacrament. Let me thirst to share You with others, in my love for them, in my accepting them as they are, in my forgiving them. Let me thirst that all the world will know You — and the Father, through You.

John 4:5-42

Your enemies, Jesus, prided themselves on their faith in God, but it was only pride in the faith they had in the god which they had created for themselves. Pride is always the biggest obstacle in my loving You fully, because I've read and studied a lot, because I am a religious, because I pray a lot, and because I work a lot. I sometimes think that is all I need to possess You.

But I need to look at You always as a little child — full of trust and love.

I need to be simple.

I need to recognize You in every gesture, word and action of everyone I know and meet. I need to find You in the blowing wind, in the bright stars, in the flowers and warmth of the sun.

I need to know You in the depths of my being.

I need to trust my whole life to You; to let go of everything, to let You be in me.

Luke 4:24-30

When I think of all the things I have been forgiven by You, my God, I know that there are so many I couldn't make a list of them. You have forgiven me everything, and more than seven times seventy. Give me a forgiving heart like yours. I resent some people who get on my nerves, who say and do things that irritate me, even when they mean no harm. I remember people who in ages past have hurt me. How can I expect Your forgiveness, unless I forgive and accept others. But I can't do it in my sinful weakness.

I ask You to give me the help, the strength, I need.

I ask You to give me the heart of Jesus,
   so I can forgive and love others with His
   heart.

From this moment, in His heart, I do forgive and will learn to love.

Matthew 18:21-35

March 28

We sometimes forget, Lord, that others expect — even unconsciously — to see Jesus Christ in us. They expect us to be loving and attentive and caring, as Jesus was. He wasn't afraid to be in the company of women, to visit their homes. He wasn't even afraid to be with sinners and tax collectors — and not because He was superhuman; He wanted to teach us how to teach others about loving God. People seldom learn about loving You through books or lectures; they learn it by loving others, by seeing how others love You in those around them.

Let our lives be the books we write.
Let our loving communities be the light
that warms the hearts of those who meet
us. Let Your presence drive out fear
and draw others to love You.

Matthew 5:17-19

It is a divided world we live in; the forces of good and evil struggle in every possible way to attract the spirits of God's creatures. Through our religious commitment, we accept the fact that we are on the side of good. Lord, by the power of Your Spirit, help us to exorcise our own house, to drive out of ourselves all the weaknesses we cling to. At least let us hold firm to the desire and intention of doing Your will in all things. As we try to fight the forces of evil in the world, we must first intend to conquer them in ourselves. Teach us to support one another in the battle, to encourage one another in hope, and to love one another, that hatred, darkness, and evil may be overcome.

Luke 11:14-23

March 30

Jesus, the greatest thing You taught, the
greatest commandment, the summary of what
life here on this earth is all about, permeates
my life and every moment of it. It is no use
writing it above my doorpost, or even tracing it
in the palm of my hand. I need it written in my
heart, so I won't forget, won't sin against it.
I have to remind myself all the time that this is
what You call me to. I fail every day in some
way. But thanks to Your help I begin again. I
discover some ways I have been offending
against this greatest commandment that I
never noticed. That is Your grace, too. Please
be patient with me, stay with me always to
teach me again and again to love You above all
things, and to love everyone as I love myself.

Mark 12:28-34

March 31

The most certain indication that I'm filled with pride is the hurt I feel when others ignore me, don't give me the praise I expect, don't listen to me, and a million other humiliations. How can I be rid of such an ugly vice?
Jesus, I will keep studying Your life, as You humbled Yourself for love of me; I will remember Mary, my mother, who was filled with Your Spirit and knew that all her gifts, all of her beautiful person belonged to God. Teach me to accept all criticism with thanksgiving, as something I deserve. Teach me to use all talents You have given me, as Your precious gifts; all good is from You. Let me know who I am — Your creature, doing Your work, walking in Your steps, for Your honor and glory, not for my own.

Luke 18:9-14

April 1

Jesus, thank You for Your Word in the
readings this day. We marvel at the many
lessons we can learn from listening to the story of
the man born blind. How grateful he was to
You! What a gift of faith You gave him through
this miracle!

We ask You to heal our blindness, too. We
were born that way with the effects of Original
sin — with the human weakness that has always
been with us. We have seen only the outward
appearance of others; we can never look into the
heart of anyone. And we often judge by outward
appearance. There is no reason for us to judge
anyone at any time.

Let us see others and all events in our lives
with Your eyes. Let us understand others and
love them with Your heart. Our blindness will
soon leave us, if we always look at others the way
You look at us.

John 9:1-41

J esus, help us to grow in faith more during this
season of Lent. Everyone whose life You
touched in healing, had faith in You and was
given an even greater faith. You have touched
our lives over and over during this day, during
our lifetime. We have fed on Your body and
blood in the Eucharist; we have been forgiven
our sins merely by turning to You in faith. We
have been encouraged in our work during the
day by the support from those we live with and
work with; we have trusted that we would come
to this moment of the day to worship You again.
We know You look on us with love. Let our faith
in You deepen; we put our lives in Your hands,
we entrust to You all of the problems in our lives.
All of our relatives and friends. We thank You
again for the total gift of faith You have given us.

John 4:43-54

J esus, sometimes it is depressing to think of all the failures I have had in my life. The dreams I once had of being a saint, of doing all things in union with the will of God, seem far away — impossible dreams. But then I know how foolish it is to think such things, how foolish it is to remember past sins that have long ago been forgiven and forgotten by You. I realize how foolish it is to think about the problems that face me now or will be in front of me tomorrow. I do believe in Your love for me, and that You and I together can face any problem or any temptation. Let me trust in Your strength in me, Your presence with me. Then I can be free of useless worry and wasted depression. I embrace Your will at this moment. I will do my best to seek the kingdom of heaven first in all things.

John 5:1-3, 5-16

April 4

When I look back at the last 24 hours, I can see all of the moments when You touched my life, O Lord. Even before the light of the sun began to warm the earth, the silent trees and sky reminded me of Your presence. I sat in Your presence at prayer, embraced You in the Eucharist. I did my work and even some things I didn't want to do, which were hard to do — for love of You. I paused for a moment to think of all the people around me who were doing things for love of You and for love of others. I saw some praying, some working, some relaxing in conversations, some smiling, some bravely bearing crosses. Help me to share your love with others, by my support and encouragement, by my compassion and care, by my forgiving and loving.

John 5:17-30

April 5

Father, it would be so easy if we had written out for us every day what Your will for us is. We used to think that we could be robots — do what we were told — and it would all be solved. But we know that doing Your will must come from our own hearts, that we have to make our own decisions, our own choices, moment after moment. That means I have to reflect on Your presence in me, on what Your Spirit prompts me to do. I have to reflect and be aware of the needs of others, how I can bring Your life to others who need love, how I can lessen the burden others carry.

Teach me to say with Mary:
"Let it be done to me. . ."
Teach me to say with Jesus:
"Your will be done."
Teach me to lift others up to You,
through my love and work for them.

John 5:31-47

April 6

Jesus, You told Your disciples who had seen You that they had seen the Father, because You and the Father are one. You are God. All things are from You and in You. You are all power, all love.

Our knowledge of you — in spite of all we've read and thought of — is as nothing, compared to who You really are. The only way we can know You more is to empty our minds and hearts of all things, to remain empty, to ask You to fill us with Your presence. And then we would know You only to the extent that we could love You. Let us take many moments during the day to think of You being present, without any images or any words, just God, the Son of God, living in us. Through these moments maybe we will grow in knowledge; then we will grow in the love You want us to share with others.

John 7:1-2, 10:25-30

Jesus, Your enemies passed judgment on You, without really trying to understand what You were saying, what You were all about. You didn't correspond to their prejudices, to their pre-judgments. You didn't fit the mold they wanted to put You in.

People have done that to me and I have done that to them. I want to have the faith to forgive those who have been prejudiced toward me, and I ask to be forgiven for judging others. You are the only one who takes us all as we are. We don't fit too well into Your expectations fo us, but You forgive us and help us to become the free people, the loving people You created us to be. Let us be open enough to forgive and to accept forgiveness.

Let us be loving enough to know that only You can make all things whole, all things new. Let us be hopeful enough to know You will make all things one in Yourself.

John 7:40-53

April 8

Jesus, we know this life is often a valley of
tears. Besides pain and suffering, injustice and
poverty, we bear the sorrow of our own death
and of those we love. Even You cried at the loss
of Your friend Lazarus, for the sorrow of his
sisters. It's part of the lot we accept. And even in
the midst of our sorrow, You give us the promise
of eternal life. That sustains us; that gives us the
hope we can hang onto in this sea of sorrow that
threatens to overcome us.

Let the light of that hope be always with us,
when darkness comes. We believe in Your
promise. We reach out to You for comfort. We
feel Your arm around us to console us.
We are given strength in knowing and believing
that You are the resurrection and the life.

John 11:1-45

April 9

Jesus, what presumption it is for any of us to accuse another of being a sinner! You, who never sinned, would not condemn. You gently instructed: Sin no more.

It is impossible for us to know the guilt of another, since we can never look into another's heart. We can never judge, yet how often we pride ourselves that others are greater sinners than we are. We have seen them.

Jesus, help me to accuse only myself, to search out those faults I hide even from myself, to know how I offend You and sin against others. I ask You to have mercy on me and free me from all sin, especially that of judging others, of accusing others, of watching others to see if they sin. Forgive me for this hypocracy.

John 8:1-11

April 10

Jesus, You have told us that everything You
did was done in the Father's will, in union with
the Father. You and the Father are one. And the
Father is with us, as You are. You taught us to
call God our Father, a parent who cares for us as
much as a mother cares for her child. Why
should I doubt, when my heart is taken up with
being busy, or being involved in worldly affairs.
being afraid and depressed?

Father, I trust in You. I don't have to worry
about tomorrow, or the darkness I have to walk
through, sometimes. Where could I go to be
forgotten by You? Where could I hide from
You? You know not only my thoughts and
feelings, but You are closer to me that I am to
myself.
    I give myself into Your hands.
        Teach me to do Your will, as Jesus did.
        Teach me to desire that above all else.

John 8:21-30

April 11

Jesus, I know that You are the Truth. You are
the Way. You are the Life. When I committed
myself to You, I had only a vague idea of what it
meant. I didn't realize how difficult it was to
choose You day after day in every circumstance,
to choose You as the Way, Truth, Life. It takes a
lot of practice, and I hope that by the end of my
life I will be free, with the freedom only You can
give.

The challenge You give us is exciting.
Sometimes it means letting go and forgetting
those things I want for myself. It means
overcoming sometimes my natural inclinations.
It means dying a little every day. I thank You for
the opportunity You have offered me, for the
help You give me each day, for Your words
which sustain me and give me hope, for the
Eucharist which strengthens me. Thank You
for showing me the Truth, which is Your
presence within me.

John 8:31-42

Jesus, show us the Father, I know it is impossible for me to know God, as He is. Sometimes I try to capture His omnipotence in my small imagination. My thoughts can reach out beyond what I see, past all the known universe; they could go forever into space — and never touch the knowledge of God. But, Jesus, I can capture You in Your history on this earth, in Your words which You shared with me, in Your Spirit which You have sent to teach us. All of the things I know from that experience tell me something about the Father.

It is enough to keep me busy praying and loving for the rest of my life.

Fill me, through the Spirit, with that knowledge.

Fill me with love, that it may embrace every human person, every created thing.

For it is only through total and complete love
that I can know what it means
to be called a child of God.

John 8:51-59

April 13

Jesus, it is only through the gift of faith You
gave us that we can believe that God became
man. Without faith, it would be impossible for
us to even think of such an extraordinary thing.
How could God so humble himself to take on
this flesh which is so susceptible to cold, heat,
hunger, pain and death! How could God so love
us sinful creatures! To become like us. To live
among us. To die for us. I believe; help the
weakness of my faith.

Jesus, I want to be involved in Your passion
and death. All the pain, sickness, guilt, and
sorrow of my life I want to unite to Yours.
Accept me as part of Your life and death.
    It is the way You redeem me;
        it is the way You, Son of God,
            redeem the world.

John 10:31-42

April 14

Jesus, it was ironic that Your enemies thought that by killing You, they would save their own lives. It is ironic, that we who believe in You, sometimes think that there is life apart from You. As we walk with You through the days of Lent and the events of Holy Week, let our hearts be changed. Let our minds be full of wisdom; let our lives be united with Yours, so that we will never choose anything that separates us from You.

Your enemies made the decision to put You to death. You knew there was very little time to finish what You had to say and do. You continued to reach out to Your friends and disciples, to support them, to reassure them, to bind them to the truth. Renew us in that way these days. Let us stay close to You in our work and prayer. Let us share with You the threats and the vision. Let us also accept whatever is the will of God for us.

John 11:45-57

April 15

Jesus, how different it would have been, if the
crowds welcoming You into Jerusalem had had
the courage to follow You all the way, if the
leaders of the people had believed and been
faithful to You. There have been times in my
own life, when I have welcomed You with
hosannas as my personal Saviour, as my Lord
and Master. But as regular as a heart beat, I can
forget You, too. I can keep You in a corner and
do what I want to do, just for myself. I can be
resentful, angry, jealous, and hurtful towards
others. You know how unfaithful I have been
and am. But the very thought of Your passion
and death have given me hope. I want to keep
my eyes on You
    especially during this time of great grace;
        I want to remember that You are suffering
           for me
             and for my sins.
I want to remember that if I forget all things and
follow You . . . I hope to share in the light of Your
resurrection.

Matthew 21:1-11

April 16

Jesus, when I think of Mary, who anointed Your feet, I think of the great and complete love she had for You. She knew who You were. She knew also that she would find You in the poor, the hungry, suffering. You are the only one we can love without any hint of self-seeking. When we love You, we must give all we are, all we have totally — willing to share in Your suffering, Your poverty, Your doing the will of the Father, without any thought of gaining anything in return. We must want only the opportunity to serve You and to love You. That is the way Mary loved You; it is the only way You can be loved.

Help me to let go of everything else and to love You in others — without self-seeking, without wanting to be loved in return. It is the way You are calling me every day of my life. Let me anoint Your feet in my service of others.

John 12:1-11

Jesus, it is easy for me to identify with St Peter, who was so confident that he would stand by You, but You predicted his betrayal. He was afraid of the suffering he would face, maybe even death. When the moment came for him to be tested, he didn't have the courage. But there would come a time, when Peter suffered for You almost daily, when he gave his life in Your name.

Jesus, I'm still like the Peter of before your death and resurrection.
I promise I'll be faithful,
    but I fall into sin.
I say I'll give my life for You,
    but I have denied You often.
Give me the courage to do what my heart wants.
It isn't at all easy
    to do Your will in all things, to deny my own
        self to follow You.
In Your mercy, hear me.
    With Your presence, I can choose
        in every instance to live and die
            for love of You.

John 13:21-33, 36-38

Jesus, You said about Judas, that it would have been better if he hadn't been born. He must have handed himself over to the devil, when he rejected You and hated Your teaching. How could I say that this same thing won't happen to me? I beg You now: let me die, rather than turn against You or betray You.

I pray You to have mercy on all people who haven't had the chance to know You and believe in You. I ask Your mercy for all who love themselves more than they love You. I beg You in my own sinfulness to give another chance to those who have turned away from You in despair or hate. Help me to love everyone in such a way that my loving will help them not to sin or fall away from You. Forgive me for those I've hurt, or didn't love for Your sake, for those I've caused to sin by my words or actions. Jesus, our Saviour, have mercy on all the world.

Matthew 26:14-25

April 19

J esus, the Jews who first believed in You were
unafraid of any threats that were made against
them. They had perfect assurance that You
would protect them in every way and give them
the confidence always to proclaim Your name.
When we grow tired or indifferent, or distracted
in doing all things for God's honor and glory,
remind us through Your Spirit of what You have
called us to do, of what You have called us to be.

Make us more conscious every day
that we are destined to proclaim
and show forth Your power and presence
to all around us.

Acts 4:23-31

April 20

Jesus, since the beginning, Your followers
have tried to imitate Your life on earth, the life of
sharing with others, of calling nothing their
own. They were loving and courageous people
who lived as one family with Your presence at its
center. Renew all of us in that Spirit. Remind us
of how brief this life is, that we have no lasting
dwelling on this earth, that all we have is merely
passing. Teach us again to let go,
   to share,
      to give of ourselves for love of You,
         and love of our brothers and sisters.

Acts 4:32-37

April 21

Jesus, we thank You for giving us the example of the apostles who preach Your Word without fear, who suffered and were persecuted but never hesitated to continue the work You had given them to do. Let us take that example into our own life.

It happens to us that we often miss
   opportunities to preach Your Word by
      helping others,
   giving our time and attention to others,
   by giving our own good example of loving
      service.
Help us to recognize
   the chances we have to do these things.
Give us that grace.
   Move us by Your Spirit.

Acts 5:17-26

I run with the disciples to the empty tomb. It is a hollow place, an empty place. But there is still a warmth in the air, where You have been. I know and I believe that You have risen from the dead. And I believe that in You, I shall have eternal life.

Jesus, let me walk with You during these days of Easter, remembering Your death and resurrection each time I receive Your body and blood in the Eucharist. Fill me with the light of Your presence at that moment.
In this earthy vessel,
    let me carry You carefully,
        sharing Your love and light
            with those around me.

I thank You for the gift of faith that You have given to all those who believe in You, especially for all the newly baptized. I pray that through their lives they may bring others to love and serve You.

John 20:1-9

April 23

J esus, I rejoice in the joy of the women who
met You on the road after Your resurrection.
How happy they were that You had come back
to them! They remembered all You were to
them — You who had taught them to call God,
"Our Father," You who had said that if they
believed in You, they would have eternal life.
Meeting You was a moment when they knew
that they would never be without the joy of
knowing You.

Jesus, let that same joy be in my heart always.
I know that there will be trials and failures, there
will be times of darkness and loss, but deep in my
heart I will keep that space where the joy of Your
resurrection will be my most treasured memory.
I hope and pray not to let go of it,
no matter how long or difficult the way
to eternal life.

Matthew 28:8-15

Jesus, sometimes I have felt that I had lost
You, as Mary Magdala felt, before You found
her after the resurrection. Once I wrote:

> Where were you, Love, today?

> I looked for You in the early morning
> in Your Word
> in memory and longings for yesterday

> I looked for You on the mountain
> in Your extravagant creation —
> pine trees, massive crumbling rocks,
> slender flowers, purple and yellow.

> In the vastness of Your world
> and in my mind, I found only doubts
> and fears. These, of my own undoing,
> I offered You.

> Where were You, Love, in my looking?
> Where shall I find You to hold You forever?
> Shall I wait
> until You find me?
> You are my shepherd.
> Call my name;
> I'll run to You.

John 20:11-18

April 25

Jesus, You sent Your disciples into the whole
world to preach in Your name, and You
supported them by the signs and wonders they
worked. It was through the signs and wonders
that many came to believe in You. On this feast
of the Evangelist, St Mark, we pray that our
faith may be increased through the sign of Your
love for us which we see in our own lives.

Você have supported us so often when we
    failed you,
you have forgiven us;
    you have loved us deeply through others;
you have called us to follow You in religious
    life.
We believe; help our unbelief.

Mark 16:15-20

E ven when You appeared to Your disciples
after the resurrection and showed them Your
wounds, they were slow to believe. But You
opened their minds, so the truth became clear to
them. They were overcome with joy.

Jesus, sometimes all things seem to be clear to
me. I know and I believe that You are the Son of
God, that You are present in all who believe in
You. I am so convinced that for a moment I can
truly say with all my heart: My God and My All.
Thank You, for those moments. But I ask You
not to let my faith weaken in those times when
You seem far away, in those moments when I
forget You, or even try to put other things in the
place where You should be. Let me always be
certain that deep within me, You are present in
the darkness, in the forgetting. I know You are.
Jesus, Son of God,
    have mercy on me, a sinner.

Luke 24:35-48

Jesus, when You stood on the shore and looked at Your beloved fishermen who didn't at first recognize You, You must have been thinking of the future joy and glory they would experience. But they had a long way to go, before they would come to You in eternal life.

Jesus, You have shown us Your glory in so many small ways. Sometimes we recognize it, and sometimes we don't. You gave us the promise of eternal life. Sometimes we long for that day; sometimes we don't. Teach us to have our hearts set on You. Every day let us hear You calling us from the shore. It is possible that we can see beyond what we are doing, to that distant light which beckons us. We have a long way to go, and a hard one, but the joy You have promised is a small burning within us that draws us on and will someday lead us to You.

Thank You, our Saviour and Redeemer.

John 21:1-14

Jesus, the disciples whom Mary Magdala told of Your resurrection, didn't believe her. I suppose they thought she had been imagining it. They probably didn't realize the deep love she had for You — a love that could not be deceived. Your appearance to her confirmed her faith; the image of Your glorified body would be with her forever; everything she saw and knew would be in that memory, that presence of You.

Teach me to see things in the same way — in You, to see all of those around me in You, especially, the lonely, the needy, the rejected, the hurting. All things show forth Your glory, but above all, those You loved most, while You were on this earth. Open my eyes and heart to Your beautiful presence in everyone and in every thing I meet.

Mark 16:9-15

"Blessed are they who have not seen and believed."

Jesus, we do believe that You are the Christ, the Son of God. We haven't had the advantage of knowing You when You lived here, died, and rose from the dead. But You came to us — You chose to come to us — in our baptism, in the faith which You gave us freely without our seeing. We have come to know You: Your presence in the Sacraments, Your presence in ourselves, Your presence in all those who believe in You.

Jesus, help that gift of faith to grow in us. We ask that every day there will be some growth, some revelation in our lives of faith. We want to be aware always that You are alive in the world and in us.
    Though doubts must come to us,
        though we are often guilty of lack of trust,
            we beg You to see us through the darkness
                of those times.
    Give us Your mercy and gently lead us
        into the fullness of eternal light.

John 20:19-31

J esus, we have been re-born through our
baptism, with water and the Spirit. But we
realize that we must continue to be born again;
we need the renewal that only Your Spirit can
bring us, and we will continue to need healing
and renewal for the rest of our lives.

We ask You to teach us to recognize the signs
of Your Spirit's presence — that breath which
breathes where it will — in this world. It is
through Your Spirit that we love one another —
let us know that, and be renewed with every sign
of love. We are moved by Your Spirit in
forgiving others; let us accept that cooling,
healing wind and be renewed, and pray for those
who have injured us. In Your Spirit, we come
many times a day to pray to Our Father. Send
Your Spirit upon us, that we might be taken up
in prayer, our hearts and minds filled with the
awareness of God's presence. We ask to be
reborn, so that we live and move and have our
being in You.

John 3:1-8

May 1

Jesus, how blessed was Your foster-father, Joseph. He was beloved by Mary and by You. He was chosen by our heavenly Father to be Your protector and Mary's. His creative talents were known to many, and You were known as the carpenter's son. But few knew who he really was, as few knew who You were.

Joseph was, at his center, a man of Faith, a man of God. Against all reason, he believed the word that was spoken to him in dreams and visions. He knew in his heart that his Creator spoke, and he didn't hesitate to respond fully to doing God's will.

Jesus, teach us to remember Joseph, to learn how to trust in God's love for us. Let us believe fully in God's Word. Let us trust. Take from us that impatience which wants answers here and now. Let us wait upon You. Teach us
　　to be still,
　　　　to listen,
　　　　　　to dream.

Matthew 13:54-58

May 2

Jesus, You came into the world to bring Your light into our darkness, to drive out all darkness and make all light. We want to step out of our own darkness into Your light. Our hearts are sometimes full of shadows, the darkness of our pride, our self-love, our dislike of others and their ways. Our hearts are as changeable as the night and day. We open ourselves to You and enjoy the warmth of Your presence; then we cover ourselves with our own sins and hide from You.

Take possession of us. Lead us to dare to live fully in Your light, let it shine through us and drive out all the shadows we are accustomed to cling to. You have chosen us to be with You as the light of the world. If we live in You, and You live in us, we can let our light shine; we can love others with Your love; we can share Your peace with others; we can give light to others, so they, too, can drive out the darkness of this world.

John 3:16-21

May 3

J esus, we believe that You and the Father are one. We believe that, when we worship You, we worship the Father and the Spirit. We believe that when we ask the Father anything in Your name, we will be given it. But we often have some hesitation. When we ask to be saved, to be forgiven our sins, we know that You hear us and answer us. But when we ask for spiritual or bodily healings for ourselves and others; when we ask to be rid of some temptation or burden, we are hesitant; there is a little doubt that we will be heard. We are trying to give You room to say no. We are really adding to our petition: *If this is Your will.* We pray that this isn't a sign of lack of faith. We only mean to be telling You that we trust You completely — You know what is best — we want to entrust to all of our lives and the lives of others, but we must keep asking for those things which we feel we need here and now. Make our prayers honest and unselfish; make our trust full and complete.

John 14:6-14

Jesus, I praise and thank You, for Your compassion for the poor and hungry. Your prophetic action in multiplying the loaves and fish nourishes us every day in the Eucharist. And as we receive Your body and blood, we are reminded of those millions in the world who are hungry and starving to death. How do we reach them? How do we feed them?

Jesus, how can I eat, when someone is without any food? How can I be clothed when others are naked? How can I be comforted in my protecting room, my soft bed? I don't know an easy answer to these questions. But, Jesus, look at my willing heart. In some way, that only You can manage, let me share with those poor and hungry in this world. When I receive the Eucharist, let me be united with Your poor; let all I am, be given to those who are suffering and starving.

John 6:1-15

There have been many times in our lives
 when the seas have been rough,
 when the wind blew us away.
We have been tumbled in the breakers of
 the ocean tide
and tossed by winds of torment that Dante
 describes.
It's part of the journey.
But the intervals of peace
 are worth the frustrations, when You, Jesus,
  have been there and said:
   Don't be afraid. I'm with you.

Jesus, help us to know that, always —
 that You never leave us.
We leave you sometimes,
 but You follow us no matter where we go.
And You're there to say: Don't be afraid.
 Even when You don't seem to be near us
  or in us,
 let us believe that You are near.
Let us trust in Your love,
 let us trust in the faith You have given.
  Hold us by the hand,
   and we won't be afraid.

John 6:16-21

May 6

Jesus, no matter where we go in the world, no matter how intriguing the sights of all the natural wonders You have brought into creation, no matter how breath-taking the journey — there is nothing more wonderful in all this life than to walk with You.

We envy the disciples on the road to Emmaus, but we know we can do the same; we can be in Your presence wherever we go, we can hear You speaking to us, opening our minds and hearts.

Teach us to appreciate that other journey — the journey of Your presence in Holy Scripture. We walk with You there, in the silence of our hearts, and You draw us after You, so we are lifted up and our spirits rest with You, in the bosom of the Father. Let us never weary of the journey, but continue to seek You out, to find You, and keep You, as You have found us and revealed Yourself to us.

Luke 24:13-35

May 7

F ather, we constantly long to know Your will
for us. If we know what You want us to do,
then we hope that we will do it.

Jesus has told us that to do Your will is to
believe in Him, whom You have sent. And
believing in Him means to keep the
Commandments, to listen to His teaching, to
accept Him into our lives.

We pray for the understanding to accept
Christ into our lives. We want to be open to
His presence, so that His light floods all the
chambers of our hearts, driving out the
darkness, warming us where we have been
cold, touching us where we have been slow to
respond. Father, teach us to do Your will; to
    to know Your son,
        to live in Him and with Him,
            to accept all that He is meant to be for us.

John 6:22-29

May 8

J esus, You are our bread, our food of life.
Almost every day we feed on you;
 You become part of what we are.
   We become part of who You are.
You are the food that keeps us alive in this dark
world, that gives us strength to fight the good
fight against the enemy. You are the food that
fills us, so that we don't hunger for the food of
this world. You are the bread we contemplate,
we live with, we carry with us through the day.
You are the bread that has come down from
Heaven, to go with us on the journey, to lead
us to our true home with Your God and our
God.

 Jesus, give us a hunger for this food,
  that our hearts will long for it,
   that our bodies and spirits rejoice in it,
    that we always realize
     it is the only life we have.

John 6:30-35

Jesus, we know we can live with people for many years of our life and really not see them. We get used to them being there, to seeing them around. But sometimes it happens that we recognize them for who they are; their individuality, their goodness, their nearness to You.

And, Jesus, it happens that we are near to You many years of our lives and don't recognize who You are. We take You for granted. You are always outside of us. We really don't get to know You, for who You are. Teach us to see and to believe. Let us know what it means that You have come down from Heaven to give us eternal life.

You are the Son of the God who loves us.

You want to live in us.

Open our hearts so that we see You and know You with the love that is in us.

John 6:35-40

Our faith sometimes is taken for granted; we know we believe all that the Church teaches, but our knowledge can be just something we memorized, something we have not really learned by heart; our faith can be very shallow, and the mysteries of God can bring us darkness, instead of light.

Father, teach us to know Your Son, Jesus. Knowing Him means looking into His heart, into the mystery of who He is; it means letting ourselves get lost in that mystery. Help us that when we eat His flesh and drink His blood, we might realize how it is that we are involved in all of life, all creation, in every living thing, in every person of every time. Father, help us be rid of the darkness that covers our faith; renew us; lift us up into the light who is Your Son.

John 6:44-51

May 11

Jesus, I do believe that you live in me, and
that I live in you. There are moments when
that is all I know — and all I need to know. But
there are many times when that knowledge
seems like a foreign thing to me. It's completely
out of my mind and out of my life. It's difficult
getting back into that truth, like trying to put
on clothes that are too small or too big.

Help me, I pray, to grow into that
knowledge, before it is too late. Let it be
everything to me: that I live in You, and You
live in me. Even when I'm busy, when I'm
depressed, when I'm hurting for any reason, I
want some little part of me, at least, to
remember that You are here with me; that I
have nothing else to live for, except You, and
being with You.

John 6:52-59

Mary, this month of May has always been in a special way your month. Perhaps it is because May is so fruitful. We see growing things, blooming things; we see sun and rain bringing forth the gifts of Mother Earth.

A poet said: beauty is truth, and truth beauty. All beauty and truth remind us of your Father and our Father; they bring us closer to the Son of God, whom you brought into the world. And you yourself are mysteriously truth and beauty; you are the Immaculate One; you are the fruitful earth bringing to birth the One through whom all things came to be; you are the joyful one. Let us hold your Son in our arms and hearts during this month, and for all of our lives.

John 6:60-69

Jesus, You are the one through whom we have entered into life. You are the gate; You are the shepherd. We go through many passages in our lifetime; You are the gate of each one. You are the one through whom we entered adolescence, maturity, old age. And You will be the one through whom we will enter into the bosom of the Father.

We give ourselves into Your hands. Lead us in these days and years. Let us hear Your voice and respond to You with all of our hearts; let us run to You every day of our lives, to be led by You, to be embraced by You. You have called us by name, and we recognize only Your voice; it is the voice of love, the voice of the promise of eternal life. We are Your sheep; You are the shepherd.

John 10:1-10

May 14

Jesus, the more I remind myself that You have chosen me, the easier it is to concentrate on what I'm supposed to be doing. The temptation I have most is to think that I'm in charge of my own life, and that I must make decisions about what to do and where to do it. But if You have chosen me, then You always know the way in which I must walk. Help me to let go of my own self-will and to let You work in me, in everything I do. That isn't easy. I keep getting in the way of Your work. I'm always forgetting that You're with me and trying to lead me. Please give me an open heart so I can receive Your Word into it; give me a willing heart so I leave it in Your hands; give me the perseverance to respond to Your choice of me, for the rest of my life.

John 15:9-17

May 15

Jesus, Son of God, it is a joy for us to
remember that we are the sheep of Your flock.
We belong to You. Wherever You go, we will
follow. When You call us by name, we will
come to You. If we don't stay close to You,
then we will be lost. We will wander away; we
may even be given over to the wolves.

You see us through the dark and dangerous
valleys; you lead us to cool spring water when
the days make us weary; You comb out our
wool and pour soothing oil on scratches and
cuts we get now and then. We know You will
protect us from all dangers and lead us into
eternal life. In our small way, we try to return
the love the You show us, by pledging every
day to live and die for Your love.

John 10:22-30

May 16

Jesus, we hear You say how You search out those who are lost and bring them back to You. We see it in the lives of many of the saints. We know that Your great desire and Your Father's will is that no one be lost, that all return to You and follow Your Commandments. We pray that we continue to be converted from any habits of our lives that offend You, that are sinful. Every day we must begin again through penance and prayer to walk by the narrow way, to enter into life by the sheepgate which is You. We pray for ourselves and for all sinners in the world, that all may hear Your voice and return to You, that all may know the peace that only You have to give, that all may be saved through the precious blood which You have poured out for us in Your passion and death. Jesus, we thank You for the time You give us to repent.

Luke 15:1-10

May 17

Jesus, Your presence in the Holy Eucharist
is the most impenetrable mystery. Through the
ages people have always tried to explain it so
we could understand a little better. Now and
then, sparks of light come to us, and we say:
"Yes, I believe." We know that it isn't faith
that explains and makes clear; faith can only
say "yes" with deep devotion, because You
have said "This is my body; this is my blood."
That is all we can know, until we know You as
fully as we can in the Kingdom. So we worship
You in the Eucharist, as You are truly present.
We pray that You will be the center around
which all the world turns, that all eyes look for
You here, that all hearts worship You and find
peace in Your sacramental, Eucharistic
presence. We humbly thank You for Your gift
of this faith, for the gift of Yourself here in some
mysterious way on the altar.

Matthew 11:25-30

Jesus, it is sometimes impossible to know what reality is — what is real, and what is not real. The only reality that our hearts should long for is, that You are the Way, the Truth and the Life. And that reality is intermingled with all of the visible and material things around us, with all the emotions, desires and thoughts we have. If we could experience and make real Your presence in all of our here-and-now world, then we would never be separated from you. Keep reminding us what the reality is that we must embrace and enter into every day of our lives. When our hearts are troubled and burdened and confused, reach out to us that we may take Your hand and let You lead us where You want us to go.

Jesus, our Saviour, I implore
that I may love you more and more.

John 14:1-6

Jesus, You and the Father are one.
Everything You did and experienced on earth
tells us something about the God we worship;
we think of Your care for the little ones — the
poor, the crippled, the children, and the
rejected. It is the Father's love reaching out to
them: comforting, healing, and promising that
they shall be with Him in eternal life. And
when You died for our sins, it is the Father also
saying to us that He loves us that much, to give
us anything we need to have eternal happiness
with Him. Jesus, help us to reject anything
that keeps us from loving You with all our
hearts and souls. Let our eyes be fixed on You;
our hearts set on You. We thank You for
showing us the Father.

John 14:7-14

Jesus, You have told us many times, in many different ways, to trust in You, to have faith in You. If You had not given us that gift of faith, we would be wandering on the earth, looking for You without knowing what we were looking for. We would have been empty people, ghostly people. We treasure that gift despite all of our fickleness and all of our weakness. In this prayer, we hold that gift out to you: make it stronger, more trusting. When it is so dark that we can't see this gift within us, let us trust; let us believe. We have committed ourselves to You; we have dedicated our lives to You. And though we have failed in so many ways, so many times, we trust in Your love and forgiveness; we trust that You will renew our faith and let us be Yours in every way, forever.

John 14:1-12

May 21

Jesus, You have told me that saying "I love You" isn't enough. It isn't enough to go through the motions or repeat the right words. You expect me to keep Your Word; and Your Word is to love God above all; to love others, as I love myself. Your Word must be on my lips and in my heart, every moment of the day. Your Word must dwell in me, when I'm disturbed, discouraged and doubtful. Your Word must be the light to my path, my companion, my food and drink.

I ask You to help me with Your love to be renewed in Your Word every day of my life. Teach me to begin and end the day with Your Word in my mind and heart. Your Word is my salvation, my hope and my joy.

John 14:21-26

May 22

Jesus, we live in a world that is constantly threatening our peace. We are surrounded by distractions and fears — temptations that are capable of destroying our peace. You are the only security we have for our defense, for our protection. Give us Your peace. Fill us with that trust in Your proven love for us, that we won't be afraid, that we can face any danger. We know that our own strength, our own confidence, is not enough. We rely only on You, and we trust completely in You, so that we can always possess Your peace deep in our hearts.

John 14:27-31

May 23

How often, Jesus, I have thought that I could do something on my own, that I had to bear burdens with my own power. It is impossible to bear any fruit apart from You. There have been moments of success and moments of pleasure, when I have thought I had achieved something, but then came the knowledge that all without You is ashes.

There is no life, apart from You.
Renew in me the life that only You can give
to those who remain close to You,
who live in You.

I pray You to dwell in me and work in me the work that You want done. For any fruit that is born through me is started by You and brought to fulfillment by You. I am useless and barren without Your life in me. Thank You for this day and for Your coming into the world through me.

John 15:1-8

May 24

Jesus, the sign of those who love You and
keep Your word, is joy. It is the emotion we
feel, when we think of the eternal life You have
promised. It is the result of the love that we
have for You and for one another. But You
give us a bonus for that kind of joy: You show
us the reflection of Your presence in the world,
in all created things, especially in all people
who are created in the image of God. It is a joy
to know that You are alive in the world — in
Your creation and in the spirit of love that You
send into the hearts of those who believe in
You. Let the joy we experience pour like a
river, into the communities we live in, into the
world we love in Your name.

John 15:9-11

May 25

Jesus, when I look at my own sinfulness, my
weakness, my infidelities, I can hardly believe
that You will do with me what You will.
friends. I am not worthy of Your love. But I
believe, because You have said so, and I want
to try my best to live up to the love You have
for me, the love You show to me by choosing
me to bear fruit in this world.
The very thought of Your loving me
is enough to make me love everyone in this
world;
it is enough to let me bear with patience
all of the troubles that this life brings;
it is enough to cause me to pray to You
that You will do with me what You will.

Your choice of me was from all eternity,
and I ask that You protect me,
from anything that would cause it
not to continue into eternal life.

John 15:12-17

May 26

Jesus, You told us that a servant is not greater than the master. Sometimes we have forgotten that when the way has been too demanding, when life has become so completely frustrating. Whatever You suffered, we can suffer, too, according to our limited capacities. Teach us to remember that whatever physical pains or moral trials we are faced with, we stand in Your name, we bear them in union with You. Let us have generous hearts, so we can be worthy of the name that we have gotten from You. Teach us to rejoice in whatever things we must suffer, so that Your name will be glorified. There is no greater victory than having Your will be done in us.

John 15:18-21

May 27

Jesus, we know we are not orphaned. You have sent us the Paraclete to remain in us. But we do live in an alien world; we are foreigners and strangers in a land that does not know You. At times, we feel helpless, when we see all of the injustice that exists in the world — the killing, the starvation, the poverty, the greed for power and pleasure that fills the hearts of so many. We know that only You can change things. And we pray to You for all those who suffer. We ask You to send Your spirit of consolation and hope into their hearts. Let them not be bitter and despairing, but give them the hope to persevere and await Your coming, when You will give justice and glory to those who have suffered in Your name.

John 14:15-21

May 28

Jesus, we thank You for the Spirit of Truth,
which You have sent into the world.
Sometimes we have hoped that the world
would be changed in the twinkling of an eye,
but we know in our hearts and are grateful for
the Spirit who lives so fruitfully in the remnant.
Those who believe in You, and to whom You
have sent Your Spirit, must be immoveable
witnesses to Your presence in the world.

Help us to be faithful.
Each day is a challenge
to be a faithful witness to you.
We want to keep the memory of You
close to our hearts
and express it, teach it, with all of our
words and actions.
We thank You for the Spirit of Truth
that will always be a light
in this dark world.

John 15:26—16:4

L ord, we pray You to increase the work of
Your Holy Spirit in the world. We know that it
is only through the gifts of the Spirit, that all
people can come to You,
> can learn to love one another freely and
> with joy,
> can appreciate the gift of eternal life that
> You have promised all those who
> believe in You.

Send Your Spirit into our hearts at this
moment to inspire each of us to abide in Your
love. Make us instruments of Your peace.
> Through Your Spirit, we can heal
> those who are hurting,
> those who are afraid,
> those who are without hope.

Fill all of us with Your Spirit,
> that as we worship You in prayer,
> our hearts, minds, and bodies will be
> rededicated to do and be in every
> moment of our lives
> what You have willed for us.

John 16:5-11

May 30

Jesus, so often we have longed to see You, to
be with You, to know You, even as those early
disciples were with You. You tell us that the
Spirit will teach us the full truth, and that the
truth He teaches is from You, who share it with
the Father. Help us to listen and to learn. The
unthinkable *is* possible for us in this world: to
know You, to know the Father. When we seek
You alone, we will find You. When we put
everything else aside, out of our hearts and
minds, we will find You there. When we
desire nothing except You, we will be filled
with Your presence. In everything we touch
and see and experience, we wil come into
contact with Your presence. Lord, hear our
prayer.

John 16:12-15

May 31

W hen love became incarnate, Mary carried
that Love to her cousin Elizabeth. And the
whole house was lighted with love. Elizabeth's
child stirred in her womb. Mary and Elizabeth
both were moved by the Spirit to sing their
praise of God's love for all of creation. Mary's
song was for the lowly ones: They shall be
exalted.

O Jesus, You are the Love of the world. You
give Yourself to us, so we can carry You within
us. Help us to be more conscious of that love,
so we can let others be blessed by it. Let that
love possess us, so that no other experience can
take its place.

Zephaniah 3:14-18

June 1

J esus, renew in us the virtue of hope. We
want to expect and long for and be patient in
our waiting for all those joys and blessings You
have promised. You didn't say we would be
without pain in our waiting. But often our
human weakness gets resentful. We say that it
isn't fair to be treated this way, to be given no
special sign, to see everything falling apart,
with no believable signs of Your coming. We
need hope, something to hold on to, when we
feel the beginnings of anger, when we begin to
get restless and think: what is the use of
waiting? We sometimes get like the Israelites at
the foot of the mountain — not expecting
Moses to return.

You promised, and we believe.
Come to us with that cooling balm of hope
and teach us to treasure it, hold on to it.

John 16:20-23

Jesus, we believe that the Father loves us,
because we have welcomed You into our
hearts, as our Lord and Master. You tell us to
ask Him for everything in Your name. We ask
Him to keep us from sin, to change our hearts
so that we want what He wants in everything
about our lives. We ask to see before us always,
His love, flowing like a river, so that our love
for others, our love for all of His creatures, will
be renewed and refreshed.

We ask that His love will flow from our own
hearts into the hearts of all around us,
especially those we live with and are close to.
We ask that our thoughts, words, and actions
be infused with His love, so all of the world will
be drawn to praise Him, serve Him, and love
Him.

We thank You, Jesus,
for showing us the Father
in the love You have
for the weak, the poor, and the humble.

John 16:23-28

F ather, our hearts long for that eternal life
which You promised us, in Jesus, Your Son.
You have given us the gift of life in this world.
It is good and has brought us many other gifts.
We have lived in joy in the goodness and
beauty that You have shown us in Your
creation, in other people, in ourselves. But the
gift of this life, we know and believe, is only a
shadow of the life You have promised us in
eternity. We ask You that every day we long
for it more. We ask that with every pain,
disappointment, suffering, we will let go a little
more of the life we see and touch and hold on
to. We long for the day when we can put off this
world, where we have learned to love — and
come to You, where Your love will be all in all
for us.

John 17:1-11

June 4

Jesus, You have conquered the world; there is no darkness nor evil we should fear. We need only to remain in Your presence. You have not left us alone; You are with us always.

We thank You for giving us the courage to trust in You. We have failed in many ways, but we know and believe that with trust in You, we can overcome our human weaknesses, as You overcame the world. You warned Your disciples that they would have trouble but not to be afraid. We recognize the troubles that face us, but again and again we return to You, to ask forgiveness and the strength and the trust to be more faithful, each day. Let us always have the confidence to know that at the end of the journey we will be all that You have called us to be.

John 16:29-33

June 5

Jesus, You told Your disciples that You are glorified in them. You are glorified in us, also. The disciples were the same kind of people we are; they had their weaknesses, but with their faith in You, they overcame them. They were afraid, stubborn, sometimes angry and confused, but they believed in You and in all that You taught them. They believed in You with the courage that eventually led to their martyrdom. So it has been, with all Your saints. So it is meant to be for us. Help us, Your weak children. We believe that You have given us all that is necessary to live our lives in imitation of you.

Day after day, we give our lives
    into Your hands;
help us to glorify You by our words,
    by the way we treat one another,
    by our deep desire to love you
        above all things.

John 17:1-11

onsecrate us, Jesus, in the Truth. St Paul
instructed us in this, when he said: "Put on
Jesus Christ." Every day we need to put on
Your face, Your mind and heart, Your words
and actions. Then we shall live in the truth.

If we think of the image that we are wearing,
of the person we want to project to others, then
we will live in the truth.

You prayed for us that we might be one, as
You and the Father are one.

Any division we create
is a division between us and You.
We are denying the truth.
Help us to live in Your love,
so that the union we establish in You
will not be broken even by death.
Help us not to sin against this truth
by anything we say or do.

John 17:11-19

June 7

Jesus, Your love in us is what binds us to one another and draws us every day to live in You and in the Father. The more we love one another and express that love in our words and actions — through sacrifices, forgiveness and prayer — the more the world will believe in You and know that the Father sent You into the world, the more will they know that the Father loves them and offers them eternal life. Give us the strength not to fail You in this vocation of love to which You have called us. For if we don't love one another, as You and the Father love, then we are failing in our whole reason for existing.

    Heal our broken hearts,
        renew our love of one another,
            let our lives bear the fruit of love
                which is Your presence in the world.

John 17:20-26

Jesus, if we went through this world without
loving You, then we might as well have not
lived. Even if we accomplished great things for
humanity, if we increased the growth of the arts
or sciences, and didn't love You, then we
would be nothing. You know all things; You
know we love you. Help us to grow in that love,
so that all we do will be the fruit of that love.
You know all things; You know the fruit we
bear is witness to the love we have for You. If
we love one another, if we are merciful and
forgiving, if we are rid of greed and selfishness,
then we can truly say with St Peter: You know
we love You. We offer You our hearts, put
them within Your own Sacred Heart, to learn
how to love.

John 21:15-19

Jesus, we prepare to celebrate again the coming of Your Spirit into the world. We remember the rush of wind, the tongues of fire. We remember the transformation of Your disciples who became living and courageous apostles — witnesses to Your Good News. We remember the work of Your Spirit through these centuries. We remember that You sent Your Spirit into our own lives.

Renew us now in that Same Spirit.

Give us new hearts that we may be
re-born in Your love.

Bind us to Your Gospel through Your Spirit, always to be our food and drink, that the Spirit will be our strength in the darkness, and in the fight we wage against sin. Help us to wait in longing and with courage, as we pray:

Come Holy Spirit.

John 21:10-15

Father, we thank You for the Paraclete sent to us through Your Son, Jesus, the Spirit is the Love of God.

We think of the darkness of Calvary, where Jesus died, and the light of the Pentecost room, filled with tongues of fire. We think of the suffering of Your Son and the glory given to His followers. We think of the jeers of the rabble around the Cross, and the awed silence when the disciples spoke in tongues. We have a vague knowledge of what we are, of what You have called us to be. Our journey is often one of pain and suffering, but there's a glory in us, aching to be born. We are a sinful people but a holy nation. We walk in the darkness, but the light of Your Spirit calls us to our goal. Teach us to dwell in the light, to use the gifts You have given, to rejoice always in the promises You have made.

Acts 2:1-13

Jesus, You have given us a mission to accomplish in this world: to share the gifts You have given us as Your followers. We often pretend we don't have them; we keep them for ourselves — and then wonder why they don't bear fruit. You had faith in Your disciples, that they would do as You told them to do; You have faith in us, that we will give Your peace to all we meet. But our faith is often weak; we don't understand the needs of those we meet, or remember that You have sent us to them. Remind us that we go to others in Your presence, to see them as You see them, to believe in them, as You see and know their capabilities to be what You want them to be. Let us give of ourselves to one another, that Your Word may bear fruit in the world.

Matthew 10:7-13

June 12

Jesus, out of Your love for us and Your
confidence in us, You tell us, as You told Your
disciples: We are the salt of the earth, the light
of the world. You have given us all we need, to
do the work You have called us to. Help us to
stop hiding from the challenge that faces us.
Show us how to use these gifts. Lead us to
those areas where the salt of Your Word is
needed to give hope and joy to others. Help us
show the light of Your presence to one another,
in the work we do, and wherever you let us go.
But let us treasure these gifts and build them
up with our own love for You and for others.
Jesus, let us become Your people, for You have
given us these gifts to take You into the world.

Matthew 5:13-16

Jesus, St Anthony had a burning desire to serve You by preaching to the pagans and a willingness to become a martyr — to die for love of You. But You led him in a different way. That burning love became alive in his preaching, in his writings, in his praying for miracles for the poor and humble. His intercession before Your throne is still powerful today.

We thank You for this feast that reminds us that we share doubly in his life. We ask to imitate his Franciscan way of love of others, and the total love he had for You. May we be led to imitate his willingness to follow where You lead.

II Peter 1:3-11

Jesus, it seems that we never change, that we still have the same failings and sins we had years ago. We are like the scribes and pharisees who kept going through the motions, doing their good works, saying their prayers, but not changing their hearts. Create in us new hearts! Prompt us to be more determined to overcome our habitual faults. It is not only possible; it is what You desire. Remind us that today we must become all we can be; we must become what You have called us to be, in order to enter into heaven. We know You have given us the strength to do it; we know and believe that You have given us the means to overcome the darkness in us. In Your loving way, move our wills so that we will want with all of our hearts to do Your will.

Matthew 5:20-26

June 15

Jesus, You call us to the Way — in which
there are no compromises. You told us to seek
first the Kingdom of Heaven. Forgive us for all
those weaknesses You see in our lives. We have
sinned, because we have so often thought of
ourselves first. We have been self-seeking; we
have lived often for the things of this world.
Teach us to let go. Teach us to be able to say
every day of our lives: I have nothing, I want
nothing, except You, Jesus, my Lord and
Saviour. And by possessing You, we can
possess all You want us to have; we can love
others with the same love with which we love
You; we can love ourselves because we are
loved by You. We can live and move and have
our being in Your love. Keep us, Jesus in Your
love.

Matthew 5:27-32

Jesus, some people say that the teachings You
give us about how to live are impossible to
follow. How is it possible to turn the other
cheek, when someone really hurts us? How is it
possible to love people like that? How is it
possible to give to anyone who asks? Yet we
believe that You were not exaggerating. You
meant what You said. And it *is* possible. It *is*
necessary. You are trying to teach us that we can
do much more than we think we can. You tell us
that our potential has hardly been tapped in the
way we live. We are accustomed to draw on only
a small portion of the power of our human spirits
— our trust in our own power and in the gift of
faith You have given us is often minimal. Awake
us from the false dream. Let us accept the fact
that we can do what You demand, and that You
will always be with us, as we go.

Matthew 5:33-37

T each us, Jesus, that every day of our lives we will say with conviction in all we do: "Now is the acceptable time! Now is the day of salvation!" We need to believe that this day and this moment is a time for us to act with love, hope, and joy, knowing that You are present in the moment; that You are waiting for our response of love. What tremendous opportunities await us, each day of our lives! It is really as though You have planned it all out for us. We have the choice to love or not, to forgive or not, to accept our cross or reject it, to care for others or ignore them, to serve you or to serve ourselves. Help us to sleep and arise with those words of opportunity in our hearts: Today is the day of salvation.

II Corinthians 6:1-10

ather, we are sometimes reminded to count our blessings, to recognize the gifts You have given us through Jesus Christ. It would be impossible to actually count them, for everything we have and are is a gift from You. There is nothing in our lives that has not been given. We ask Your grace to have the strength to offer all these gifts back to You, to use them for Your honor and glory, for the good of others rather than for ourselves. Too often we have squandered Your gifts on our own pleasure, for our own selfishness, without thought that we are wasting what You had given us. Renew in us the determination to give all that we are, day by day, for love of You. Help us to hold back nothing, to waste nothing of the good things You have given us.

II Corinthians 8:1-9

O ne of the rewards for serving Jesus faithfully and preaching the Gospel with all of our strength, is the peace and joy of Christ, which is given to all of those who do this. We read of how Paul and Barnabas and the other Apostles rejoiced in their persecutions, since that was a sign that they were making progress in disseminating the Gospel. Today, we know that the worst thing that can happen to the Christian community is to be sunk into a state of apathy and indifference. We know from our own experience that is the worst thing that can happen in our own spiritual lives.

Father, we pray You that we may not be so indifferent as not to respond everyday to Your presence, that through our prayers and sacrifices we may bring the peace and joy of the Gospel to all those around us.

Acts 13:44-52

P aul warns the Corinthians that they could be seduced by false prophets and taken away from Christ. Jesus, we know that this possibility exists for us all of our life long. We see all around us the seduction of the world which calls to us, and intimates to us that we can love the world *and* love You, too. You Yourself have told us differently; we can't serve the world and belong to You. We ask You to let us see how we try to do both. We pray You to take from us the desire to hold on to those things which don't belong to You. We ask that You will teach us to be determined to deny ourselves, to take up our cross, and to follow You. It is only by keeping our gaze on You at all times that we can overcome the dangers that the spirit of the world offers us.

II Corinthians 11:1-11

Jesus, when St Paul poured out his heart to the early Christians, saying all the things he had suffered and done for the Gospel, we know that he did it not to brag, but to assure those who heard him that his life was totally given to You. When we read those things Paul did, it makes us feel that we have done nothing at all. However, we know that we are not saved by what we do but by faith and Your goodness. We want to offer to You all that we are and all that we do; we know that You can change our activities into things that are worthy of You. We know we have done very little, but we also know that Your love for us is greater than we can imagine. Give us the faith to trust You with all of our hearts; we know and believe that You will bring us to eternal life.

II Corinthians 11:18, 21-30

Jesus, we can see clearly how the Spirit led St
Paul from a life of a persecutor of the Church,
to one of Your greatest servants and workers of
the Gospel. Paul tells us that when he is
powerless, then he is strong. Teach us to know
that lesson and to practice it. When we are
weak, then we are strong. When we recognize
the fact that we can do nothing good of
ourselves, but only through Your grace, then
we know that the human weaknesses we bear
and work with all of our strength to overcome,
will become the trophies we can boast of. We
know that You call us to trust totally in You
and in Your grace. There is nothing we can
depend on in this life, except Your presence,
Your love of us, and the gift of Yourself to us.

II Corinthians 12:1-10

June 23

Jesus, we always rejoice in the way the Spirit
led the early preachers of the Gospel. The
Spirit moved their hearts not to put obstacles in
the way of the Gentiles so that they could find
You, their Lord and Saviour. Teach us again
their example. Send Your Spirit into our
hearts, so that we can see where we do prevent
others from coming to You. Sometimes by our
bad example we put up blocks to Your grace;
    sometimes it is by our self-righteousness;
    sometimes it is by ignoring others,
        pretending that they don't exist.
    Enlighten our minds and hearts
    that we might better understand our role in
        the world;
            all of us who have been given the
                gift of faith are meant to share it
                    with others;
if it isn't used, we know it will die.

Acts 15:7-21

Father, today we celebrate the birth of St
John the Baptizer and reflect on all the
marvelous things which surrounded his birth
and his life. He was a special person from the
very beginning, for his role in life was to
prepare the way of the Lord.

   Help us to realize that You also picked each
of us for a special life to live,
       for a particular role in life.
You chose us to be born into this world;
       You graced us with believe in Your Son,
           Jesus;
You even called us to follow You
       in our particular vocations.
Renew us now in that life You chose for us. We
have had many false turnings in our life;
we have failed, sometimes miserably, so we
need to be renewed, called again, redirected to
fulfill more perfectly the role You have planned
for us.
   We ask You, Jesus, for this grace.

Luke 1:57-68

ather, we thank You for the way Your
Spirit led the apostles, and especially Paul and
Luke, to preach Jesus' Word among the
Gentiles. The Spirit led them by visions and
direct intervention to where You wanted them
to be. The Spirit prevented them from going
wherever it would do them harm.

Let us respond to Your Spirit in the same
way as they did.

There are times when we don't hear Your
Spirit, speaking to us; teach us to listen to
everyone, and everything in our lives that
speaks to us in Your Spirit. For there are times
when *we* go places that can only do us harm.
Let us recognize Your Spirit, warning us and
guiding us away from harmful places. Each
day we pray that we will be open with all of our
hearts, to the words and guidance of Your
Spirit.

Acts 16:1-10

June 26

L uke tells us that the convert named Lydia
was one who *listened* to what Paul was
preaching about Jesus. When we think of
ourselves and the thousands of sermons we
have heard during our lives, we wonder if we
have ever heard all that was being said.
Obviously, we have heard some of it, or we
wouldn't be here. But if we had heard and
responded to it all, as Lydia did, we probably
would be caught up in the Spirit, whenever we
heard the Word of God preached. Father, we
ask You again to send Your Spirit into our
hearts that we may never hear a sermon, or
read Your Word, without responding in a way
that will change our lives and bring us closer to
You.

Acts 16:11-15

June 27

When Paul preached to the pagan Greeks he
spoke from the depth of his heart, as one who
had experienced the same things they did —
initial disbelieve that Jesus rose from the dead
and doubt that God was revealed in this way.
But he also spoke as one who had come to
believe that God had made Himself known.
Our faith has been given to us as a free gift. But
it is a gift that, we have often been reminded, is
meant to grow, deepen, and finally take total
possession of us. We are called every day to
acknowledge what we believe, to live out what
we believe. Our faith must be shown not only
in our trust in God and dependence upon Him,
but it must be shown in our living the Gospel of
love, it must be shown in our love of one
another. Jesus give us this renewal and this
grace!

Acts 17:15, 22—28:1

June 28

J esus, You said to Your followers that they
were "weak in faith." You said this because
they thought that they were responsible for all
that happened in their lives. They had no trust
in the heavenly Father's love and care for them.
They could not understand how it was
humanly possible to be totally dependent upon
God's will and providence.

Jesus, we can relate to these disciples,
because we have the same trouble. We think
that it is necessary for us to provide for
ourselves in all things; we seem to think that
God doesn't know what we need. We have to
keep telling Him, because we seem to think He
is blind or deaf and doesn't understand what
goes on here in this life. Help us to be more
trusting in His providence.
Help us to take more risks,
to let go of our security,
to give ourselves more totally into Your care.
Increase our faith and trust.

Luke 12:22-31

June 29

The Spirit of the Lord rests upon us. We are told that God does provide a way back for the sinner; that we can have hope in Him. Sometimes it seems that our failures pile up and up and become an almost senseless, unbearable burden. We are weighed down so much at times that we might be inclined to say there isn't any hope for us. But we are reminded that God never lets go of us; we are never considered useless (as we sometimes think of ourselves); we see His miracles for the sinners in the Gospel; we remember how He sought out sinners to be with them. And so we continue to hope that we will always belong to Him, and that our offenses will be few.

Psalm 32

June 30

Jesus, Lord, we ask You to teach us to be
generous with You. All that we have of life,
and love and blessing, we have received from
the Father through You. We get wrapped up in
the gift sometimes, and think more of that than
we think of You, or why You have given us the
gift. We thank You for all the gifts we use each
day to do our ordinary works. We praise You
for them and offer them back to You. We thank
You for the love that You have let us share with
others of family and friends; we praise You for
that and will endeavor to use it for Your honor
and glory. Whatever we have is Yours; we
want to be generous in using it to praise You,
but if You will be pleased by taking it from us,
then we offer it freely, without regret, out of
love for You.

John 13:33-35

J esus, we are members of Your Body; we live in You, and You live in us. We are the church, the same church that You promised to build upon the Rock You called Peter. Let us always be faithful to Your teachings, faithful to the Holy Spirit which breathes in the church. We are grateful with all of our hearts for the gift of faith You have given us, for the baptism, the confirmation, You called us to in the church. Teach us not to hoard this gift, but to share it in all we do and all we are with those around us. We pray that every relationship, every contact we have with other people, will be inspired with the Spirit. We pray that all people will be brought fully into Your body, that all will come to believe in you, the one true Son of God,

> who came for our salvation
> and eternal life.

Matthew 16:13-19

July 2

J esus, sometimes in our lives we tend to live
as robots; we like to plan out everything there
is to do for every day for every year — just the
way we think it ought to be. But we know it is
impossible to choose to follow You, once and
for all, without any doubt, without any
indecision. Every day we have to choose You
and Your way and Your teaching, above all
else. You call us to that. When we live by the
spirit of Your love within us, when love of You
is the touchstone against which we match all
our choices, then we know we're going the only
way we can go. Following You is not easy, but
it is the only way that brings our hearts peace.
We stretch out our hands to you: hold us
firmly, that we follow You, no matter what the
cost.

Matthew 8:18-22

July 3

M y Lord and my God! I believe in You. I say
that easily — too easily — when things are
going along without any difficulty, when things
are going the way I want them to go. But when
I get no consolation from prayer, when prayer
is nothing but distractions, my heart remains
cold, when I say: My Lord and my God. When
I get sick, or someone I love is suffering, when
my plans blow up in my face, and I don't know
where to turn, then trusting You is the hardest
thing I've ever had to do. I pray that someday
You will lift me into a complete and confirmed
faith, so I will know and believe. Let me mean
it with all of my heart, when I say, "I put all
things, all my life, all of the world into Your
hands." Hear my prayer, my Lord and my
God.

John 20:24-29

Jesus, You have power over all things. When Your disciples doubted or were ineffectual in working signs and wonders, You told them that they were weak in faith, that someday they would do greater things. Jesus, we have faith, and we believe that You will help us drive away all those evil harassments which hinder us from coming to You and serving You fully. We are full of distractions; we sometime set our hearts on completely selfish things; we are taken over by anger, resentment, jealousy and envy. Help us to cast them out and set us free. Help us to be vigilant and not entertain any thoughts that are not of You, that we will be the temples of Your Spirit that You and the Father and the Spirit will dwell deep within us and enable us to live for peace, justice, and freedom for all the world.

Matthew 8:28-34

July 5

J esus, we know that sin is the only thing
that can paralyze us on our journey with You.
One of the problems is that we can foster a
habit of sin in our lives that we don't recognize
after a time. We can grow selfish in little ways,
putting ourselves first on most occasions. We
treat those we live with as the Other, not like a
person but like a thing. We can hoard our time
and energy to be used just for ourselves and our
own occupations.

   Jesus, we ask You to heal us:
            open our eyes,
            open our hearts,
            teach us to recognize Your presence
            in everyone else, to love and respect
                them.
            Then our love will no longer be
                paralyzed
            but will come alive and grow.

                                Matthew 9:1-8

Jesus, when I hear that You have come to call sinners, I know You have come to earth to save me. From birth and the Sacrament of Baptism, You have claimed me, but I have sinned all along the way. I have stumbled and fallen. I have lived for myself.

Let me focus again my eyes on You;
let me set my heart on You;
let me walk faithfully in the way
You have shown me;
let me recognize my sinfulness,
so I can be free of it.

You are generous in forgiving;
You are graceful in always accepting me again into Your own heart.

I need You with me every moment;
I need to love You above all things.

Matthew 9:9-13

July 7

Jesus, You have recreated us over and over;
You have made us new; You have filled us with
the wine of Your presence. You have called us
to fast — not in the sterile, deadly way — but
in the way that brings growth. You have called
us to abstain from our selfishness, to put away
from ourselves any lack of love, to become
empty in our hearts, of all those things we are
attached to, which hinder us from loving You
and loving others. That is the only fasting that
is pleasing to You.

Give us the gift of this kind of fasting,
so we will continue to be renewed,
so we will be generous in serving You,
so we will be Your servants
in re-creating the world.

Matthew 9:14-17

July 8

Jesus, I have often been weary and burdened
in the many years of my life. I have, at times,
found the world too much, too meaningless, too
painful to want to go on. But at such times —
though they seemed to last for an eternity —
You did come to me with Your light and Your
comfort. I pray to You now that I may more
readily recognize Your love, Your gentleness,
Your patience with me. I know and believe
You love me. I know there is no darkness and
no burden that can separate me from You.
Help me to hang on to that trust, when my life
is bleak. You are the only God, the only Lord,
the only Saviour, I have or want.

Matthew 11:25-30

Jesus, when we walk with You in the memory of Your miracles and see You raise the dead to life, see the people with trust in You be healed, we rejoice in Your goodness! And we keep saying: "Do it again." Our hearts are united with Yours, for we want all hurting people to be healed. We give You thanks for letting us share in those times of so long ago.

We ask You to let us continue to share in Your desire for all things in this world to be right. We want to seek with You: peace and justice, the sharing of wealth, the improvement of the lost of the poor, of prisoners, the neglected sick. We unite our hearts with Yours; we unite our faith with Yours. We unite our energy with Yours and will continue to work for a world that is pleasing to You, where all people are treated with justice and love.

Matthew 9:18-26

Jesus, the harvest is too much for those who have been called to bring the Good News to all the world. So we pray as You told us to pray, to the Father for an increase of laborers. We pray, first of all, that those whom You call to religious life and the priesthood, will respond to that call, helped by our example and prayer. We pray, further, that the Church will begin to use all of those qualified people who have not been invited to preach the Gospel and administer the Sacraments. And, finally, we pray for ourselves that we may be constantly aware of the opportunities we have to do more, to be more, to give more, so the Good News will truly be good, in the way we live it and preach it.

Matthew 9:32-38

July 11

Jesus, help us to use the time we spend with others in the way that will bring Your presence to them. Sometimes we just have to listen to them, for so many people need only this — to share their thoughts and experiences with others. Sometimes, we must comfort them, as we often have thought of comforting You in Your long passion and suffering. Sometimes we have to show our love in our words and actions, touching them, holding them in our arms. Be with us, loving Saviour, wherever we go, to visit, or to work, so that we ourselves will be confident of Your presence and that others will experience Your presence with us.

Matthew 10:1-7

July 12

Jesus, we pray that we may be the light of the world that You intend us to be. We know that You use the faith of those who believe in You to spread Your Kingdom, to bring the gift of faith to others. We ask You to forgive us for all the ways we turn people off, for keeping them at a distance, for not always seeing You in the rejected of this world, the poor, the vagabonds, sinners and the sick. There have been times when we, perhaps unconsciously, felt that others were not good enough for us to bother about. Forgive us for distorting Your Image, that others are seeking and need. Help us always to preach Your Gospel, by who we are.

Matthew 10:7-15

Jesus, we pray for all Christians who have gone away from their homelands to bear witness to You. We can't really experience the loneliness, the deprivations, and the persecutions that they often suffer. We ask You to give them courage, to give them the grace to persevere, to be near them, so they will always draw comfort from Your presence. We pray for ourselves, too, that we will always support them with our letters, our gifts, and our prayers. We pray that You will continue to call others to preach the Gospel in this way, and for those whom You call, that they will respond wholeheartedly. We thank You, Jesus, for letting us share in some way in the works of Your missionaries in all lands.

Matthew 10:16-23

Jesus, when You say that it is enough for the disciple to become like the Master, You are expressing the vocation of all Christians. No matter where we live out our lives, we are called to the same Way, Truth, and Life. We are called to be like You.

    Teach us to speak as You spoke —
        words of love, forgiveness, healing,
        comfort.
    Teach us to go where You went —
        to the poor, helpless, discouraged,
        suffering, lonely, loveless.
    Teach us to desire what You lived for:
        to do the will of the Father in all things.
We offer You at this moment our whole lives: all we are, have and want to be.

    Love us so we will become like You.

Matthew 10:24-33

July 15

Jesus, I learned to say Your name when I
was very small. In the many years since then, I
have read about You, thought about You,
heard You talked about more times than I can
remember. But sometimes I still don't
recognize You. There have been times when I
have been sick, in pain, depressed, in trouble,
and I couldn't seem to find You. There have
been times when I have been very happy,
successful, in love, and I didn't think of You.
And I can't count the number of people I've
turned away from, avoided, ignored, because I
didn't recognize You there.

Please help me. Renew me. Open my eyes
and my heart, so I can find You — in myself,
first of all, in all the events of my own life, and
so I can find You in others and all things in
You. Unless You show me and teach me, I will
never learn. I put all my trust in You.

Luke 24:13-35

July 16

The apostles were accused of filling Jerusalem with their teaching about Jesus. How powerful was their faith! How great the Spirit of God, working in them! We can imagine the thousands of believers who followed after them, to hear more. How wonderful it would be, if we could imitate them, by filling the world with the name of Jesus.

Jesus, stir up our faith, so that through our prayers and good works we might be instruments in bringing others to hear of You and believe in You.

Acts 5:27-33

July 17

This world is full of miracles:
happenings that are strange and wonderful.
We live with them, we touch them,
we have found them in our own lives.
On the other hand, there is a world
full of suffering, pain and injustice,
that miracles have not come near.
We live in a world of broken dreams.

    Jesus, we ask You to let us bring into this
darkness, the light of Your life. We don't
understand the mystery, but we have faith in
You, hope in Your promises. Let us share that
faith and hope with others, through our love.
You are the miracle that is alive in this world.
We come to You, to heal all the brokenness, all
the pain, all injustice. We believe in You;
hear us.

Matthew 11:20-24

July 18

There's a dream we have, of coming into the presence of God. Perhaps we would disintegrate. But it's a dream that You, Father, created in us from the beginning. So we know that one day it will come true, and You Yourself will protect us from Your majesty. In this life, we find You in Your Son, Jesus. He is Your living Word, taking possession of our minds and hearts. He is Your gift of life, gift of food, gift of making us what we eat. In knowing Him, we know Your love. In loving Him, we prepare ourselves for the entry on our final earthly day into Your awesome presence. Father, we praise You and give You thanks.

Matthew 11:25-27

Jesus, Son of God, in You is our peace. We have had some miserable times in our lives — wandering in darkness, away from You, not being able to understand that You were anywhere near. We finally came to our senses and came to You. You healed us. We have carried burdens of sorrow and pain and frustration for long periods; we screamed and cried, we even cursed at times. We came to You, and You took our burdens and pain and frustration upon Yourself. At this moment, we are a bit weary with all of the work and confusion, but we know that we can put it all into, Your hands, and it will be all right. Jesus, Son of God, You alone are our peace.

Matthew 11:28-30

J esus, we are so quick to judge others,
especially when we see someone breaking the
rules, or a law or custom. At least to ourselves,
we say that they are wrong, they are sinning.
You, the Master of the Sabbath, never judged
others in that way. You offered mercy, instead.

 Teach us to do the same.
 Teach us to accept everyone as they are,
  to love everyone just as they are,
  to give You thanks for anything anyone
   does,
  knowing that You alone are Lord and
   Judge.
 And we thank You for being merciful to us,
the greatest of sinners.

Matthew 12:1-8

Jesus, You said that You came to call
sinners. Crowds of them came to You, to be
healed, and many stayed to follow You — some
all the way to death. But many refused to hear
You, because they thought themselves saved
without You. Let us look into Your face and
confess our sinfulness, our selfishness.
Sometimes our pride prevents us.
Remove that darkness;
turn us around to face You.
Let us see how we hurt others,
then call us to come to You,
so we can rejoice in Your presence
in ourselves and in others.

Matthew 12:14-21

July 22

Father, we thank You for the gift of love that
You have given Your creatures. We realize
that the variations of love are almost infinite,
but we are convinced that Your
Commandments of loving God and loving our
neighbors, aren't some intellectual exercise.
We know we can't be human, until we have
loved.

    We ask You to let us overcome
the reluctance to show our love of others,
to overcome the pride that keeps us
from taking the risk of loving.
It is only through loving in a human way
that we will come to recognize You
as the Lord, as Mary Magdala did.
Help us to come to You and to cling to You,
Our Lord and Master.

John 20:11-18

Jesus, You are the only sign we need —
the sign of the way we are to live. You are the
ultimate sign of the Father's love for us.
Sometimes we have been tempted to question,
to doubt. We have even thought, at times, that
You didn't hear our prayers; You didn't care.
All You ask of us is to trust You completely, to
put aside our self-seeking and enter into Your
life, especially to put ourselves into Your
suffering, and to be still. You will do all that is
necessary for us — if we but wait and trust. Give
us the patience; give us the peace to be still
and trust You.

Matthew 12:38-42

Jesus, the only lifestyle that binds us to You, is doing the will of the Father in heaven. If we could only get it all together, every moment of the day and night, choosing always and correctly to do God's will, we would have a deep peace that nothing could take from us. The trouble is, we don't always choose in that fashion. We let ourselves get in the way, our desires and remembrance of pleasures, and we choose our own wills.

> Give us the courage and the wisdom
> to do what You want us to do.
> We want nothing more
> than to be totally Yours.

Matthew 12:46-50

July 25

Jesus, we marvel at what happened to the
disciples, after they met and followed You. If
they had not responded to Your call, we would
never had heard of them. But they did respond.
And they all became more than ten feet tall,
more than they could have otherwise hoped.
They displayed gifts that no one, not even they,
dreamed they had.

   You have called us in the same fashion.
You have called us to be
      the light that shines in the world;
You have called us for others.
      Let us not hide ourselves and our gifts
      under our private bushels.
Let us use all of our ordinary gifts
      in extraordinary ways
      for Your honor and glory.

Matthew 20:20-28

July 26

Jesus, sometimes I imagine what it would be like, if I had not been born into a believing family and been given the gift of faith in You. I've met many men and women who don't have that gift. Some are decent people; some are apparently not. Some believe in our Father, but not in You; some believe in nothing, except this world and this life.

I ask two favors in this prayer: Increase my faith, that I may live and be Your love for others. And secondly, I pray for all those who don't believe, that they may be given — in Your mercy — the gift of faith, to bring them into Your eternal Kingdom.

Matthew 13:16-17

July 27

J esus, we thank You for choosing us as the
good soil, for sowing Your Word in our hearts.
We can hardly say that we have borne the fruit
so abundantly, so beautifully as we wished, but
we have been as faithful to Your Word, as our
sinful condition allows. Every day we ask You
to renew us in Your Word, to infuse more life
into us, to bless the fruit we bear. We need
Your Word to speak through us to others, with
love, encouragement and forgiveness. We need
Your life, to make us aware of those people and
those places where our talents are needed. We
need Your blessing on our work, so it will be
purified and solely for Your honor and glory.
We thank You and rejoice in Your love.

Matthew 13:18-23

July 28

Jesus, it is easy for us to see that we live in a
world that is both good and evil, full of saints
and sinners, believers and unbelievers. You say
of Yourself, that You came to call sinners to
follow You, and that is the vocation to which
You have called us. We can't be satisfied with
worrying about our own growth, or comforted
by our life of prayer, not when there are
multitudes who need You.

Send Your Spirit into our lives, to show us
where You want us to be at this time in our
lives. Take away from us any indifference we
have toward those who are physically, morally,
economically in need.

Matthew 13:24-30

We read, Lord, of the meeting tent where You came to speak with Your prophet Moses. How blessed he was! How the people honored him, who was given this great gift to speak to You, the Lord and Master of all creation! How blessed we are to be ourselves Your dwelling place! Our persons are the meeting tents where You dwell, where we can be aware of Your presence; this is a holy place where we dwell, in which we live all of our lives on this earth. Let us be aware of this sacred place and of Your presence, not only that we are the dwelling place, but that many around us are likewise blessed by having You live in them. Let us honor them and give them the respect due to this dignity of being Your tent, Your tabernacle, Your temple.

Exodus 33:7-11, 34:5-9

Jesus, when we read Your parables today,
they seem easy to understand. You have given
us centuries of knowledge, and Your own
Spirit to help us understand. How can we
praise You and give You thanks for this sign of
Your great love? As You speak to us
in the Gospels, we want to treasure Your
words, we want them to be living in us, we
want to show that life in all we think, do, and
say.

Help us do that.
Help us to begin today, to begin again,
in living Your Word in our own
communities,
in speaking that word to all we meet and
work with.

Matthew 30:31-35

July 31

Jesus, teach us to imitate the positive
example and spirit of the early followers of
Your teaching and Your way. We see how
the apostles sent missionaries to rectify the
incorrect teaching that had been given to the
Gentiles. The apostles saw how necessary it
was to avoid putting needless obstacles in the
way of others. You taught that Yourself, when
You accused the Pharisees of laying burdens on
others that had nothing to do with their love of
God and their salvation. Let us realize that
such things are not pleasing to God, that
insisting upon our own rule for others can bring
harm to their spiritual lives and may even kill
their spirit. Let us truly appreciate
Your mercy, love, and generosity,
so we can share it with others.

Acts 15:22-31

Lord God, how You must tire of Your
servants, when we think we are burdened
beyond our strength! Moses almost broke
down completely under the burden of his work
in leading Your people, but he didn't
understand that he wasn't carrying this people
by himself. Without You, nothing can be done.

So often, Lord, we forget all about You and
thank that we are in complete control of our
lives and of the whole world. We ask You to
give us the consciousness of Your work and
presence in our lives. Let us know that
everything that happens in our lives happens
through Your power and begins and ends in
You. Let us offer every moment of our lives to
You for Your honor and glory, so You will be
praised forever.

Numbers 11:4-15

ather, give us the strength to promote peace and justice in the world, as best as we can. We recognize how many millions throughout the world and in our own country are exploited, are treated unfairly. We think of this, when we hear the instructions You gave Your chosen people — to be fair and honest. But we know that we first have to be this way in our own lives, in dealing with one another, in our speech and actions if we are to have an influence on others, if we are to have the slightest impact on the world. Let us reflect Your justice in our work, our prayers, and in all of our relationships with others.

Leviticus 25:1, 8-17

J esus, we ask You to lessen our pride. It is so foolish for us to be proud of any thing we have or anything we are. Antying that is good about us, came from You. We have nothing that we haven't been given. We remember how You were insulted in Your home town, because you were a carpenter's son. We insult You, too, when we think ourselves better than others, because of the free gifts You have given us. We ask forgiveness for those times we have been proud. We ask forgiveness of those whom we have looked down upon; we open our hearts to You and ask You to empty them of sin. Fill them with Your love, to teach us to be the servants of all others.

Matthew 13:54-58

Jesus, we thank You for the example of John
the Baptist. From the very beginning of his life,
he was prepared for his mission. He prepared
the way for You into the hearts of many people.
His life ended early, as Yours did, from the
hatred others had for him.

Help us to renew our dedication to You.
We have been destined to be Yours
from the moment of our baptism;
we have been called and called again
to follow You.
Let us keep hearing Your voice
and responding to it.
Let us accept our mission day by day,
even when it means dying a little to ourselves
and dying to this world.

Matthew 14:1-12

August 5

The vision of Daniel tells us in another way, what Mark tells us in the story of Jesus' transfiguration. In Daniel's story, Jesus is given the dominion, glory, and Kingship that is due Him, as the Son of God and the Redeemer of all peoples of all times.

Almighty God, we honor You and praise You for this revelation of who Jesus is. In spite of knowing that He has this place of honor in the Kingdom of heaven, we are still limited in our knowledge and understanding. Our minds cannot reach the limits we would need to reach, in knowing You, and Your Son, Jesus. But we thank You for what You have permitted us to understand. And we long for the day when we will be fully enveloped into Your presence at the end of our lives here. Help us to live always for that promise and according to Your will.

Daniel 7:9-14

August 6

Jesus, it is good for us to be here. It is good to be in Your presence at any time, but to know You through the eyes of faith in the Eucharist, to relax and be silent in Your presence within us, to be reverent of Your presence in others is the kind of good that only You could give us.

We thank You, for all of those moments. Help us to build a sacred place in our lives, where we will always be drawn to remember, to worship, to be renewed in love for You which we can bring into the lives of others and into the darkness of this world.

Mark 9:2-10

L ord, at times we are afraid. There are a lot of things in this life which frighten us. Sometimes we are afraid that the end of the world may come through devastating wars and weapons. We are afraid that our faith may grow cold, and we will live in a darkness that can't be overcome. We are often afraid because of our past sins.

Help us to be not afraid, but to trust totally in Your love and mercy. Increase our faith in You, so we will have a secret joy within us, knowing that You desire our salvation even more than we do, that You love us more than we can imagine, that You forgive our sins more than we deserve. We thank You for telling us to be not afraid.

Matthew 14:22-36

August 8

Lord God, we thank You for the life of Saint
Dominic and for the lives of all those followers of
his who have lighted the church and world
through all of these centuries.

When we consider such people as St Dominic,
we get some hint of the potential that lies in the
depths of human nature. We realize that we
waste a lot of the gifts that You have given us,
Lord, through our laziness, our love of pleasure
and ease, our resistance to Your holy will. We
beg You, that we will respond to Your gifts more
fully, and prepare ourselves with greater
discipline to imitate those saints whom You give
us as examples.

Matthew 15:21-28

August 9

Jesus, You are the Christ, the Son of the living God. How wonderful are those words! They are like oil poured out — an assertion of all that we believe. They are the statement of our trust, our hope and our love. Let those words be our light in the darkness, let them be the sword that cuts through all doubt and confusion, let them be our consolation when we are suffering.

You are the Christ, through Whom we were brought into existence. You are the Son of God, who died for our sins. You are the Christ, with Whom we always have communion. You are the Son of God, Who promised to bring us to the Father. We offer You all of our lives and long for Your gift of eternal life.

Matthew 16:13-23

August 10

Jesus, sometimes we worry about what is
going to happen to Your Church; we are often
afraid of changes that we don't understand. We
know that it is foolish to worry, when You have
said that You will be with those who believe in
You, until the end of time. When we think of
some of the holy giants of the past, we
understand how foolish our fears are. You
always raise up those teachers and preachers
who lead believers in the right way. Sometimes
they are accepted by those they come to serve;
sometimes they're not understood until long
after their deaths. Help us to be patient, to
realize deep in our hearts that You have all of
creation in the palm of Your hand, that even the
things we don't understand or appreciate can
bring you honor and glory and provide the
salvation of souls.

Matthew 15:21-28

Lord God, we see how You gave Moses and Your chosen people a rule of life to follow and a reason for living good and holy lives. We thank You and praise You for the tradition that has directed the lives of the Jewish people from that day to this. One generation has passed on to the next a deep love of their history and a faithfulness to Your commands. We pray that we may be as conscious as they, of the necessity to pass on to those who come after us the traditions that we have inherited from our communities and from the church. Teach us that we are links in the chain that must remain unbroken. And the stronger and more loving we are, the better for those who come after us. Thank You, Lord, for all Your gifts.

Deuteronomy 4:32-40

L ord, Creator of all things, we praise You for the life of St Maximilian and for raising him up as an example to be imitated by all who believe in Jesus Christ. We beg you to help us attain some of the virtues he demonstrated in his life; especially, the generous love he had for others, even to the point of offering his life for them. Help us to care so little for ourselves, that the lives of others are more important than our own. Help us grow in holiness and to give our lives completely for love of You, Our Lord and Master.

John 14:25-27

August 13

L ord God, we have to remind ourselves very
often that everything we have, and all that has
happened to us that has brought us nearer to
You, has come from Your hand. We must
remember, as the Israelites had to be reminded,
that we are totally and completely dependent on
You and on Your will for us. Let us, then, seek
Your will, long for Your will to be done, try our
best with all of our strength to do Your will in all
things. At this moment, we again offer ourselves
to You with all we have and all we are. We throw
ourselves into Your hands. This is where we
long to be always; this is where we take our rest.

Joshua 24:1-13

Joshua told his people to turn from false gods and turn their hearts to the Lord God, who brought them out of Egypt and gave them a land to dwell in. Almighty God, we need to do that ourselves, all during our lives. Too often we get involved in using false gods, creatures that take us away from You. We don't realize that we give You only the externals in our lives; we have not always turned our hearts to You. Help us now to be converted again, to turn again, and empty our hearts of anything keeping us from loving You totally. Thank You, Lord, for this gift and grace.

Joshua 24:14-29

August 15

Jesus, we know that those who are sent by You cannot fail in the work You have given them to do. The apostles followed Your instructions to the letter and as a result many marvelous things were accomplished. Help us always to do as You tell us. But help us first to listen to what You are saying. Sometimes we get confused and what we hear is only our own voices; we are following our own hearts; we are doing our own will. We pray that You will give us the courage to come closer to You so we may listen properly and hear what You are saying to us. When things go wrong, when what we intend doesn't come out the way it is meant to then, perhaps we should think we are not doing it Your way but our way. We ask You for the grace and the insight we need.

Mark 6:7-13

August 16

F ather, we read how Your people Israel
followed false gods, generation after generation,
returning to You only when You raised up a just
judge, to lead them and instruct them. All of us
humans are inclined to be our own judges, to
listen to our own thoughts and feelings, without
discerning if we are responding to Your teaching
and the teaching of Your Son Jesus. Help us to
form our consciences on what You tell us, how
You lead us by Your Spirit. From our past
experience and the experience of the Israelites,
we should realize that on our own we will not do
what is pleasing to You. But we need Your grace
and guidance to do Your will. Give us strength
to respond to Your grace.

Judges 2:11-19

August 17

F ather, sometimes we can sympathize with
Gideon who said to Your angel that if You are
with us, why are these bad things happening?
Sometimes we are inclined to see the evil in the
world and even in our own lives as a sign of Your
absence or Your lack of concern for us and for
the world. Help us to understand that You are
always within reach, even though our lives and
the world gets dark at times, and it seems
impossible that You haven't forgotten Your
creation but are still concerned. Help us to
respond to You, by offering ourselves to You
without any conditions. Teach us to listen to
Your voice and to be responsive to the working
of Your Spirit in the world and in us.

Judges 6:11-24

Lord, we see often in the history of Your people, how You have raised up prophets to warn Your people of the dangers that could happen to them, if they follow the wrong course of action. In this time and day, we also need Your prophets — to lead us and to tell us what way You want us to follow. We realize that You can lead each of us by the working of Your Holy Spirit, but it is easy for us to be confused and to be lead astray by the false prophets that live among us. We ask You to truly send Your Spirit, which we can recognize, so that we can discern under His guidance what is right and good and follow it with all of our hearts. We trust You and believe that You will continue to guide Your people in the world.

Judges 9:6-15

August 19

L ord, Your Scriptures give us some strange accounts of the way people have responded to Your will. Such things as Jephthah, offering his daughter as sacrifice are things that we cannot understand. We realize that You worked with people at the place where they live, according to their own traditions. Today, where there is a greater respect for human life in most cultures, we ask that You continue to build up in us that love for Your image in all peoples. Help those who are persecuted in all countries because of their social condition, race, creed, or whatever brings others to kill and torture them. Strengthen us to suffer with them through penance and prayer.

Judges 11:29-39

August 20

Father, we are rewarded with the story of Ruth, the ancestor of Jesus, and Naomi, her mother-in-law. Such love and devotion is an example of the kind of love of others that You taught us in the Old Testament, and more especially in the words of Your Son Jesus. Teach us over and over to learn that lesson of love, that we love not only those who are related to us, or of the same community, but that we love especially those who need our love, or are in need of someone to help them and take care of them. It is easy for us sinners to love only those who do us good, or who can be of service to us, but this is not the Christian kind of love You taught us. We ask for Your grace to open our hearts all the way to others.

Ruth 1:1, 3-6, 15-16, 22

Jesus, teach us who are called to bear witness
to Your life, death, and resurrection, that we do
it not for our own glory or reward, but that You
might be known and loved. Let us realize that
we are preaching You, and not ourselves. It is
often a great temptation to take pride in what
others think of us, because we are good
Christians, of how they respond to our needs by
sacrificing for our benefits. Let us never think
that we are deserving of all the good things
others do for us in Your name. Help us to never
forget that people are good to us for Your sake,
for love of You. Help us to be the same in our
response to others, that we love them and treat
them well, for love of You and not for love of
ourselves. Thank You, for Your help to live
according to Your will.

I Thessalonians 5:12-18

J esus, we thank You for all of those people in the early days of the Church who responded so thoroughly to the words preached by prophets like St Paul. We know that he was successful in getting the Thessalonians to listen to Your Words and to follow in the faith. We ask You to send Your Spirit to renew our faith. We get so accustomed to saying the same prayers, to following the same routine in our worship, and living out the faith, that we forget the necessity for zeal and enthusiasm for the life that You have given us. Help us, before we lose the faith altogether. We thank You for this grace.

I Thessalonians 1:2-5, 8-10

August 23

Jesus, St Paul gives us a lesson of how we
ourselves are called to share our faith with
others. He draws attention to the way he was
gentle and loving toward those to whom he
preached, even willing to lay down his life for
them. We who are members of Your body, are
called to show that same kind of love, especially
to unbelievers and those who have no God to
listen to, or love. Help us to reach out to them, in
whatever way we can. So many millions still live
and die, without knowing anything of the
Gospel, while we remain silent in so many ways,
when we could open our lives to others. Give us
the insight to hear what You are telling us in the
letters of St Paul.

I Thessalonians 2:1-8

F ather, we thank You again for all of those apostles, who are such great examples for our own lives. We thank You today for Bartholomew, or Nathaniel, and for the openness he showed in his life, coming to Jesus with the acceptance that whatever He would tell him was the truth. And as we learn from the tradition of the church, Bartholomew was given the opportunity to suffer and die in Arabia, in witness to the faith.

We pray You to give us the renewed determination to live our faith as a witness to others, so that those who know us or hear us will not be led astray, but will be drawn nearer and closer to You. We ask that our example will be that which brings many others to know You and to serve You, even as the lives of the apostles did.

Revelation 21:9-14

F ather, all I have comes from You. I haven't always used the gifts You have given me in the right way, for the right reasons. Often I have used them in selfish ways, for my own good and glory. I want to offer them all to You at this moment. You have given me the greatest gift of all: Your own Son Jesus Christ, for my salvation. Let me give myself totally to You, in every moment; whatever I do, let it be done for Your praise and worship. Let me never cease thanking You, for all the gifts of Your creation.

Luke 19:12-19

ife is a brief moment — a precious moment.
God gives a different gift of life to each of us. No
matter how vastly different our lives are, they
are meant as moments. We return to him,
saying: I did it all for You. Father, we ask for
that grace to live our lives graciously, to be
loving, forgiving, caring, and kind. Let our lives
be a moment of glory for honoring You. Let us
unite ourselves to Jesus Christ, to show others
Your love.

Matthew 6:17-29

Lord, we put so many obstacles in the way of our coming to You. Our pious practices and prayers are often a stumbling block, because we can do them all externally, while our hearts remain blind. We want to say it is part of our human weakness, but Jesus reminds us that we are responsible for our own blindness.

We ak You to open our eyes and our hearts
and the doors of Your Kingdom.
Let our prayers come from our hearts;
let us seek You and find You,
wherever we look and in everything we do.
Let our hearts be set on You
with all of our strength.

Matthew 23:13-22

Jesus, sometimes I worry more about what others think of me than about what You think of me. I give a lot of importance to appearances; I don't want anyone to know the inside of me, what I am really like, the part of me that only You know. My prayer is that You will give me the grace to change interiorly, that I will be more concerned to change the way I truly am, to become what You really want me to be.

My prayer is for a more mature set of values, for less concern about what others see or think, to desire and strive fully to be what You expected me to become, when You called me.

Matthew 23:23-26

F ather, we thank You for the person of John the Baptist. We rejoice in the role he played in preparing the way for Christ, Your Son. We see that he put his whole heart and soul in preaching to those who would respond to Jesus. And we know that he would not back down or limit his fervor, out of fear of persecution or pain.

Help us to respond to Your call in the same way — that we not let any human weakness keep us from preaching the Gospel and living the faith in the way You have called us. Forgive us our sins, but especially let us continue to be strong in the way we live the life which You have given us.

Matthew 23:27-32

Jesus, I think often of the moment of dying, of that inevitable time when my life here on earth ends. The good moments of those reflections bring me a longing to be with You, to experience the total love of which this world's loving is only a shadow. At times I have sinned and in my guilt am afraid of dying. But my faith in Your love and mercy renews my love for You and again makes me know that You alone are everything to me. Let me look and long for that day; loving this life with its good and bad, for love of You.

Matthew 24:42-51

L ord, what can I do now to prepare for the coming of the Kingdom? I have never done any great work or anything spectacular. I have never done anything saintly. As I await Your coming, I can do only the ordinary, sometimes monotonous things that my life offers. But I can do those things in a special way, for love of You. My conversations, my work, my meeting others, my compassion for the suffering of the world, my prayer, my loving others — are all done as though they are the last things I will do, and I offer them to You today, tomorrow, and all the tomorrows of my life.

Matthew 25:1-13

September 1

Jesus, You often told Your listeners not to be afraid. For those who believe in You, who hope for Your Kingdom, there is no reason to be afraid. There is nothing in this world that we need be afraid of losing. Whatever is good and beautiful in this world, we will find in Your Kingdom. Whatever is evil in this world will be changed or cease to exist. Help us never to be afraid, not even afraid of losing You; increase our faith that we can always rejoice that we have left all things to follow You.

Luke 12:32-34

September 2

F ather, we can never tire of worshipping You,
or be forgetful about praying to You. If we forget
You, we might as well forget to live and breathe.
For You are everything to us. Wherever we
look, we see only those things which have been
created by Your hands. Whatever we experience
is a reminder that we came from Your hands and
are destined to return to You. There is not a
thought we have that is not somehow related to
You. You are our life and our being. And we
know You love us, in spite of the failures we
have, in spite of the sins we have. We throw
ourselves on Your mercy, and You will hear us
and heal us and love us, so we can be more
prayerful in all we do, and more fruitful in the
work You have given us to accomplish.

Psalm 92

September 3

Jesus, we pray for all those people in the world who are starving, who die without knowing the goodness life can offer, who have no work in which to rejoice and be glad. Hear our prayer
    that those who have more,
        will share with those who have less,
    that we will share what we have
        with those in need,
    that we will find ways of helping
        the unfortunate in the world,
        that we will seek them out.
For where we meet the poor and suffering in the world, is the place where we meet You.

Jesus, we thank You for the way You lead us to do the Father's will.

Matthew 6:31-34

Jesus, You cast out unclean spirits of all kinds; You healed wounded hearts and brought light to those filled with darkness. I ask You to let Your light shine in my heart always; strengthen me to refuse those harmful impulses that try to take possession of me. I pray that You send Your Spirit into my heart and into the hearts of all those I know — enlighten us, guide us, let us live in the freedom of the Children of God, and give us the determination to live our lives for You alone, for the honor and glory of our Father in heaven.

Luke 4:31-37

September 5

J esus, teach me to have the kind of
compassion You had for the sick and suffering.
Let me respond to their loneliness and fear.
Though I can't give them the healing that only
You can give, I can offer them my attention, my
time, my praying with them. I can assure them
that they are not alone, that my own love for
them is only a shadowy reflection of Your love
for them. Give me the strength to hold them in
the darkness of their suffering and share their
pain with them, the best I can.

Luke 4:38-44

September 6

Jesus, teach me to let go of my own plans for my life and the lives of others. I want to believe that You have a better plan for all of the things we do and are. Whenever I am disturbed and upset, because things are not going the way I want them to, let me back off, let go, and remember that You alone are in charge of my life. I want to entrust everything to You; I want to accept all things that happen to me and others, as capable of giving honor and glory to the Father. I trust You, because You love me.

Luke 5:1-11

Jesus, I know that You do not want fasting for its own sake. The only kind of fasting You desire is for me to turn away from all things that would make me lose thought of You or cause me to love You less. Fasting is good when it frees me, when it reminds me that I am not living for this world, when it gives me strength to fight the temptations of the spirit of the world. Give me the spirit of self-denial, that I will love myself and my own comfort less than I love You and love my neighbor.

Luke 5:33-39

September 8

M ary, Mother of Jesus, Mother of God, I
praise you for all of the gifts the Father gave you
and which flow in all of your words and actions.
Your virtues are like the rays of the sun falling
upon the world. They soften our hearts, lighten
our darkness, draw our thoughts and desires
toward heaven where Christ reigns. I will walk
in the light coming from you, and as I meditate
on what and who you were in this world, I pray
to become more like Your Son in all things.

Matthew 1:18-23

September 9

Everything You created, Father, is good, and
You know all things — and all of us, through
and through; there is nothing hidden or
unknown to You. The very air we breathe is
known to You and becomes the Spirit that gives
us life. We are comforted, when we realize that
You know our sins and faults and the deepest
darkness in us. You are also there, where they
are, and You forgive us and heal our weakness.
When we wander into a place that seems far
away, and we are lost, we are comforted in
knowing that You are present there, also. You
take us by the hand and lead us where You want
us to be. Even if we lived a thousand years, we
would not have the time to give you the thanks
and praise You are worthy of. We can only ask
You to accept all of our lives as belonging to
You, and wanting to be with You.

Genesis 1:1-31

September 10

Jesus, You taught us to seek the good before all else, because good is the only thing that comes from the Father. You said to us that we should seek first the Kingdom of God. There are occasions when rules and regulations bring evil into the world, when they are burdens laid upon the backs of suffering people. Let me not be so bound as to insist upon the law, when love should come first. Jesus, I praise You and thank You for loving others, rather than obeying man-made laws. Help me to understand and follow Your example.

Luke 6:6-11

September 11

J esus, we see You often with crowds of people
who are listening and being healed. We are told
that power went out from You. You have shared
that power with all who believe in You. The
same Spirit that dwelt in You, dwells in us. We
are meant to be healers of one another. Let us be
more open to Your Spirit,
    so power will flow from us
        to heal those who are upset and disturbed,
        to comfort those who are lonely and afraid,
        to reassure those who feel themselves
            unloved.
Teach us to use Your Spirit
    through our words and actions,
        from the depths of our hearts
            to be healers of all we meet.

Luke 6:12-19

Jesus, as a religious I took the vow of poverty,
but it doesn't place me among the poor and
hungry of this world. I have often lived in the
spirit of poverty, but I haven't known the
desperation and despair of the millions who are
truly without anything in this life.

> Teach me and help me
>   to let go of everything,
>   to resist the temptation
>   to acquire things, to want things.
> Teach me to set You in my empty heart
>   and to want You only —
>   to push away anything that is not You.

Luke 6:20-26

September 13

J esus, I believe that in the measure I give, it
will be given back to me, and more. I confess
that I have often given evil for evil. I have
ignored at times those who needed attention and
compassion. I have sinned in many ways against
the love that You have given me. Forgive me!
Send Your loving, gentle, accepting Spirit into
my life, so I will be to others what You have been
and are to me. There is no other way to live,
except the way that You have taught us. As I lift
my heart to You, renew it and let me share it
with all others.

Luke 6:27-38

September 14

Jesus, I know that the Cross is a symbol of the world, a world redeemed. It speaks to us of both the sorrow and the joy. The pain comes from facing up to the realities of life, from resisting the easy way. The joy comes from knowing that You walk with us and the end of the journey will bring a peace the world can't understand. Let me persevere in my halting way. Help me to keep shouldering my cross and carry it with You, the rest of the way. I thank You for showing me that I must be committed doing the Father's will.

John 3:13-17

September 15

M ary, you bore more of the suffering of this
world than even we sinners bear. You were so
united to the will of the Father and to the life of
your Son, that your heart was pierced with
sorrow. I pray to be a comfort to all who suffer at
this moment. May they be consoled by knowing
that your Son understands what they are going
through, that they are sharing in His suffering,
and that their reward will be great in the
Kingdom of Heaven.

John 19:25-27

September 16

Father, we thank You for giving us an
opportunity to know that mysterious gift of
Yours called Wisdom. Your Word speaks of it
throughout the pages of Your Holy Book. We
pray You to give us the gift of wisdom. We know
that it is only through coming to You in prayer,
that we can be filled with that wisdom. Teach us
to treasure it and cultivate it and never let it go
all of our lives, once You have shared it with us.
Our experience has often been the opposite: we
have often turned from what is wise to a passing
foolishness; we have sought pleasures, instead of
the light of Your wisdom. Now we pray You to
let Your gift of wisdom take hold of us, possess
us, and bring us to You in all we are and do.

Proverbs 10:1-14

September 17

Father, we have witnessed great disasters in our modern times: floods, wars, starvations, scenes in which bodies of human beings were piled up until death seemed unimportant. Many places in the Old Testament, we read how reverent Your people were towards all the dead. We pray that You will give us the spirit of reverence we should have and let us communicate it to others. Above all, we pray that we may also reverence the living. For if we don't love those who are alive, how can we reverence and pray for the dead? Fill our hearts with love and respect for all of Your creation. It all is beautiful; it all is a reflection of Your presence. We contemplate it with hearts full of praise.

II Chronicles 16:11-14

September 18

Jesus, we know that we can get very
impatient and even hateful under stress. Any
kind of cross that we must carry can wear us
down and cause us to return to a childish way
of behavior. This makes us aware that burdens
don't automatically bring grace. Teach us to be
open to the crosses of our life, whether they are
sudden ones or long-term ones. Help us to
accept all things as from Your hand — gently,
patiently, even with joy, if that is possible.
Take from us the inclination to revert to our
immaturity; let us grow in faith, and wisdom
with every burden, every responsibility, every
test of our faith.

Job 5:2

Father, we pray with greater concentration, when we're in trouble. And so often You have answered our prayers, in time of great need. We want to offer You thanks now, for all of the times You sent us help. We thank You for the many occasions, when You answered our prayers, and we didn't even recognize Your aid. We thank You for the help that You have given to others, when they were ready to give up and had reached the point of hopelessness. Father, You are truly loving and kind; You are merciful and always conscious of our needs. Father, we love You and thank You and praise You for answering our prayers.

Psalm 5

F ather, we praise You for all of the love that You have brought into the world in Your creation. We thank You for the love of all married couples, for the love that has brought children into the world to live for Your honor and glory, to give You praise and serve You. We thank You for the love of our parents, for the love of brothers and sisters, for the love of friends, for all the love that we have experienced for other people. Teach us that love is a holy thing, that it is Your presence which we hold in our hands and hearts and offer to others, share with others. All love is from You, and we are blessed in loving You and in loving others. Renew love in our hearts and spirits, so that it may be a light to our paths and a guide through the darkness.

Song of Solomon 2:1-7

Jesus, You have called me to follow You. I can't count the number of times I wanted to go away, to go my own way without You. I can't count the number of times I have sinned, that I have failed to live according to Your teaching and the will of the Father. But I know You have forgiven me, that You continue to reach out Your hand to lead me once again, in the way You go. Help me to concentrate always upon the Cross You carried for me, upon the Cross on which You died for my sins. I want never to turn away from it, but to embrace it every day of my life.

Matthew 9:9-13

September 22

Jesus, when I see the fruit that others bear in their lives, I feel that I haven't done anything that is good and worthy in Your sight. I am sorry for all the failures, but still I hope. I still trust in Your mercy and love. Help me to take one day at a time and to do the best I can for that day. Let me respond quickly to any word You may speak to me each day; help me to do some good thing for others each day. Strengthen me, that I might accomplish well whatever work I have for each day. Let Your gentle rain of grace fall on me, that I may grow in love of You and of all others.

Luke 8:4-15

September 23

F ather, we thank You and praise You, for all of the knowledge You have given to the human race. Through the centuries, we have grown in the knowledge of the earth, of space, of medicine, and of all other sciences. There seems at times no limit to what humans can accomplish. We ask You to let the human race continue to develop, both in the sciences that can lead to greater wisdom of the species, and also to grow in the love and knowledge of one another. You have given us life, that we might become in every way more like You. Help us to contribute to that goal by the way we live and use the knowledge life offers us, and the way that we grow in love and respect for one another.

Genesis 32:26-32

September 24

Jesus, You are the light of the world. All of us who believe in You, share in that light. Let Your light shine in my life. I ask that Your revealing light drive out all darkness that lurks in me and at times blinds me, in my attempt to follow You. I want Your light to warm my heart, so that I may love others in Your love, that I may love every one, more than I love myself. Let Your light shine through me, into the lives of others. I ask that Your light touch my ears, my eyes, my mouth — my whole self — so that I can reflect Your love.

Luke 8:16-28

F ather, Lord God, I know You are near. In the extravagance of Your creation, I'm aware of Your presence. Wherever Jesus touches my life — in prayer, in the sacraments, even in dreams — I know You are present, since Jesus reveals You to us. Since my stance in life is face to face with You, why do I find it difficult to do Your will in all things? I blink my eyes, and I have sinned; I've forgotten Your awareness of me; I've sought my own will, rather than Yours. Help me, come to my aid, hold me, so I will do Your will with all my heart and soul.

Luke 8:19-21

September 26

Jesus, I'm not called to imitate anyone; I'm
not meant to be like this saint or that one. You
have called me to be myself, as completely as
possible. If Your Word always fills my heart,
and I live by it, then I'll be everything You
want me to be. If my life is rooted and
grounded in love of God and neighbor, then I
am being what I was created for. Help me to
rid my life of all false images, to be the person
I'm supposed to be, to love You each day, in
the best way I can.

Luke 9:1-6

September 27

Jesus, since I've read the Gospels many
times, I think that I know You. But if I read
the Gospels again and again, I continually find
something new, something I had not thought of
before. You are truly ever ancient, ever new.
I'm coming to believe that I really know
nothing about You. Every day, I must begin
again to study, to pay attention. I look not only
in Scripture, but I look at the lives of others,
and I look within my own heart. I listen for
You to tell me something new. Thank You, for
letting me realize my ignorance. Take me by
the hand and lead me into Your life.

Luke 9:7-9

September 28

J esus, I should never tire of thanking You for the gift of faith. I realize that without Your plan, I could have come into the world and never heard of You, or having heard, not believed. That precious gift has helped me through many years, many trials, many wanderings. Increase my faith. Give me the opportunity to share it with others; let every action of my life express the faith I have that You, Redeemer Lord, live in me. I thank You for Your life, death, and resurrection. I thank You for my faith and the faith of all the church.

Luke 9:18-22

September 29

F ather in Heaven, You are praised, honored, glorified by all creatures You have brought into existence out of Your love. From the smallest form of matter to the unimaginable greatness of the stars, You are given praise. You are loved by all those human beings who have lived and died and now are with You, living in You. You are praised and worshipped by all those other creatures, the holy spirits we call angels. There can be no living thing that doesn't give You praise. Father, at this moment as we worship Your Son in the Holy Eucharist, let us offer You our humble praise. Let it come from the depths of our hearts and be a promise of how we want to live for the rest of our lives.

John 1:47-51

September 30

F ather, let us always sing Your praises and make known Your good works in our lives and in the lives of others. Our praise of You must be the best of all we have to offer. Sometimes we give You the least of what we have; our praise of You is often private; the honor we offer You is often secondhand, after we have honored and praised others. Help us to search our lives and our hearts, to offer You our first fruits, our most sincere love, our deepest gratitude. It profits us nothing to praise You indirectly, or with what we have left over of our energy and talent; help us praise You with our best, with every word, deed and thought.

Genesis 28:13-19

October 1

Jesus, we thank You for the life of Theresa, the Little Flower. She is a reminder to us that it isn't for everyone to accomplish some great work in the world, in order to give You praise. She is a reminder that the simple, everyday things of our lives are important in the way we do them and for the reason we do them. Theresa's life also reminds us that all life is a gift from You, and it is to You that we must offer all we do and all praise. We thank You for this day and ask You to teach us to become like little children, so we can enter into the glory of Your Kingdom.

Matthew 18:1-4

October 2

F ather, we know that eye has not seen, nor
has ear heard, the glories and marvels that
await those who belong to You, in spirit and in
truth. Your loving compassion has showered
grace upon us that we don't even recognize. We
thank You on this day for all of the ways in
which You touch our lives, in which You lead
us past permanent falls or turning away from
Your will for us. We thank You for the angels
that You have given us to watch over us. And
we believe that all of Your gifts of love are
personified by, and come through, the gift of
Yourself in Jesus Christ, Your only Son, Our
Lord.

Matthew 18:1-5, 10

October 3

Jesus, we have said that we will follow You, wherever You lead us. When we first made that commitment, we could not imagine all of the things that would happen to us along the way. How many times we were tempted to turn back! How many times we thought that You were asking too much! How many times we failed to live up to the ideal that You set for us, by Your life on earth. Let us continue to renew our choice, in spite of everything. Renew in us the spirit of Saint Francis of Assisi. Let us continue to choose You again and again, in the spirit of Francis.

Luke 9:57-62

October 4

J esus, Francis had only one book that he
desired to learn by heart: that was You, His
Lord, Jesus Christ, crucified. His heart was
the heart of a child, since this one knowledge
satisfied him completely. He studied You so
much; he loved You so much that soon You
possessed him, body and soul. How free he was
to let go of everything else in life! Jesus, teach
us on this feast day to seek nothing, except
You, our Lord. We cannot do it without Your
grace and Your support. Help us now, through
Your servant, Francis, for we have not yet
begun.

Matthew 11:25-30

October 5

J esus, when we hear You condemn the cities
that didn't respond to Your teaching or
miracles, we think that perhaps we ourselves
have not responded with as much of our lives,
as You expect of us. All of our lives we have
heard Your Word, day after day; we have
prayed and meditated. Perhaps our longing for
more, our need to be with You intimately and
every moment, is Your way of gracing us. We
pray that we will continue to respond to Your
call, that we will seek You and long for You
with all of our hearts.

Luke 10:13-16

October 6

Jesus, I thank You for the joy of the disciples, to whom You had given a share in Your power. I thank You for the assurance You gave them, that their names were inscribed in heaven — the assurance of their salvation. You have given the same promise to all of those who keep Your commandments, whose earnest desire is to do the will of the Father in heaven. You have made us one of Your own; help us to be faithful to You in all things, to keep that fire burning within our hearts, that fire which is a remembrance of Your presence and Your promise.

Luke 10:17-24

Jesus, let us respond to St. Paul's words with greater fervor than we have listened to them up to this time. He tells us that we have been called to holiness. We have heard this many times in different ways. We know that You don't want us to merely move through this life avoiding the worst of sins, but that You want us to have some burning desire to grow in holiness, every day of our lives. We have no doubt that You will give us the grace to do this; we ask that You give us the further grace to respond to Your action in our spirits. Thank You for hearing our prayer.

I Thessalonians 4:1-8

October 8

Jesus, the greatest single obstacle I have in loving my neighbor is myself. I am always giving in to selfishness, rather than making a sacrifice for my neighbor. Even when I do something for my neighbor, there is often resentment or pride. Heal me and renew me, that I may never forget that my neighbor is Your presence in the world. What I do for anyone, I do for You. When I fail others or ignore others, I fail and ignore You. Forgive me, for all the times I have failed You, all the times I hurt You in others. Thank You, for Your forgiveness.

Luke 10:25-37

October 9

Jesus, help me to tend to my own affairs and mind my own business, and stop telling others that they should do as I do. You send Your Spirit into those who believe in You, and the Spirit leads each of us as He wills. Your Spirit builds upon what gifts and inclinations the Creator has provided. I can never be the judge of others who don't conform to my way of thinking. And help me to stop condemning those who do make judgments of others. I want to listen to Your voice, to respond to Your Spirit, and to love everyone, intensely, just the way they are.

Luke 10:38-42

October 10

Father, Jesus has taught us how to pray; He gave us a special prayer, and He gave us the example of His own prayer. He said that He came to do Your will. We ask that Your will be done in us, in everyone, in all things. Help this to be the only burning desire in our hearts: to do Your will. In every work we have to do, in every relationship, in every daily plan we make, let us seek what Your will is, listen to Your Spirit guiding us, and choose to do Your will rather than our own or acting merely to please others. May Your Kingdom come, Your will be done.

Luke 11:1-4

October 11

Father, we pray that You send Your Spirit upon us. You have sent Your Spirit to us in Baptism, Confirmation, and often when we have prayed. But we need to pray always for the coming of the Spirit, until we become Yours in every way. For it is only when we are full of Your Spirit that we can fully give You the praise and glory that rightly belong to You. It is only through the Spirit that we can learn to love You and all of our neighbors with a joyful love, a patient love, a trusting love. Through Your Holy Spirit, may we lift our minds and hearts to You, every moment of our lives.

Luke 11:5-13

October 12

Jesus, in many ways and in different words
You have told us that we are either for You, or
against You. If we could see our past life clearly
and our present life plainly, perhaps we could
see a pattern that would tell us whether we are
for or against You. But that is difficult. There
have been times when we have done good;
times when we have done evil. We pray that
You will strengthen us to stand against all evil
inclinations, all evil ways of acting, so that the
whole thrust of our lives will be toward loving
You, above all things.

Luke 11:15-26

October 13

ather, through Your Word, all things were
brought into existence, and it still happens
every moment in time. Your Word formed us
and continues to shape us in the way You want
us to be. Your Word gives us spirit and life.
Help us to treasure Your Word, to listen to it
every day, to let it speak to our hearts. Fill our
minds, take us by the hand, and guide us in
Your way.

   Let Your Word bring us comfort when we
      are troubled,
  let it give us joy
     in our sharing it with others,
  let it save us, as we daily respond to it,
  and may it bring us into Your eternal
      Kingdom.

Luke 11:27-28

October 14

J esus, one of the greatest commandments
You give us, is to love one another. As St. Paul
exhorted his readers, we, too, should respond
with greater emphasis to this command. It isn't
enough just to be at peace with one another; we
should work every day to do all we can for
others, thinking of them before we think of
ourselves. Let us share our times, our
thoughts, our spirits, and our strength with one
another, especially with those who are most in
need of our help. Thank You, for all of the
graces You give us in the letters of St. Paul.

I Thessalonians 4:9-12

Father, You have sent us signs in every age. But Jesus was and is the sign from which all other saints and prophets receive the Way, the Truth and the Life. We give You praise, Father, for the sign You gave the world in the life of St. Teresa of Avila. She was born into a dark age in Christendom. She was a sign of Your power; she was a sign of the world's redemption through Jesus Christ. Help us to imitate her by using all the grace and gifts You give us. Help us all to be a sign to others, to help lead them to heaven through Your Son, Jesus Christ.

Luke 11:29-32

October 16

Jesus, I realize that one of the great
temptations and, unfortunately, sins of
Christian life is to think that I'm as good as
people want me to be. I can hide behind the
mask of righteousness, that my vocation gives
me. You have called such people *fools!* I pray
You to let the thought of what You expect of
me challenge me to try harder, to be more
sincere in my relationships, to fast and pray,
that I may be worthy of Your forgiveness.
Jesus, You are calling me to let others know me
for what I am, that I am no better than anyone,
that I have no claim to stand on a pedestal.
Jesus, help me to be what You want me to be.

Luke 11:37-41

Jesus, I ask You to let my life not be spent in going to church, let it not be spent in looking into my own heart. Let not my love for myself be mistaken as love for You. Sometimes I think I don't know where You really are. There haven't been many times in my life when I've gone looking for poor people; I haven't gone out to visit the sick and suffering, who have no one else to visit them; I haven't gone into the jails, to see prisoners. So if sometimes You seem far away, I realize that You *are* far away: you're in those places I haven't been.

Luke 11:42-46

October 18

Jesus, You sent Your disciples ahead of You,
to the places You intended to visit, to prepare
the way for You. You have called us to that
work, also. Many times when we have tried to
do that, we got nowhere. Sometimes we have
been guilty; sometimes it has been the hardness
of heart of those not believing that You would
come. We pray for all of those who heard Your
word and ignored it, for those who didn't
understand it, for those who had heard it before
and were bored by it. We pray that all of us
who believe in You, will never stop trying to
prepare the way for Your coming.

Luke 10:1-9

October 19

Jesus, You told us not to be afraid. So many times, in so many ways, You said, *Fear nothing.* We are truly free to fear nothing. There is nothing in this world that can harm us. There is nothing of the evil world that can injure us. There is nothing of the past or the future that we need be afraid of. You have saved us from our sins. You have offered us eternal life, if we will believe in You. Let us respond to Your love of us with all the love we are capable of giving. Our hearts are at peace; we live now at this moment totally in Your love.

Luke 12:1-7

October 20

Father, send Your Spirit into our hearts, that we may know at all times what You want of us. We do know what You want, but at times we get entangled in our own plans and even in our own success and forget about You. But we should know, after all this time, that if You don't build the house, then those who build it are wasting their time. Without You, nothing can prosper. So we ask You to send Your Spirit into our hearts to guide us, inspire us, stay with us, so that we will persevere always in doing what we do for Your honor and glory.

Luke 12:8-12

October 21

Father, help us to always seek and respond to Your Spirit. It is the only Spirit we can live by, the only Spirit thought which we can come to know You. If Your Spirit would take control of our lives, of our minds and spirits, then we could enter into a life of peace and fruitfulness that we have always dreamed of. Our problem often is that we resist the Spirit You send us in many ways. We know that Your Spirit comes to us through prayer, and often through other people. Help us to be open to discerning where Your Spirit comes to rest, and what the Spirit is saying to us. We have to learn to be quiet, to listen, and to judge in the depths of our hearts, how we can best seek and do Your will.

I Corinthians 2:6-13

October 22

Jesus, thank You for reminding us that the Father cares for every created thing, because all things come from His hand, because all things have been created through You, His Son. The world is holy; the world is charged with God's grandeur. And we, too, are charged with Your Spirit. We are Your people, and You are our God. All we are belongs to You. All we do is offered to You, that You may be loved and praised. Thank You for Your Gospel; every word that comes from You enlightens us and strengthens us. Your Word is our fortress, our shield, and our gateway to eternal life.

Luke 12:22-31

October 23

Jesus, in the early days of the church all those who believed in You looked each day for Your coming again, for Your triumphal reign over all of creation. Give us the gift of that same enthusiasm, the same longing that You come to claim all those who belong to You. It fills our hearts with You and our lives with good works, if we expect Your coming each day. It is as though You are already with us, within us, beside us, gently urging us to live Your life and preach Your Gospel. Thank You for this gift; continue to renew it in us.

Luke 12:35-38

October 24

Jesus, we know that You expect much of us, to whom so much has been entrusted. You called us to follow You in a special way; You have freed us from any worldly responsibilities. You have given us the time for prayer and study, the advantage of having many opportunities to praise and serve You by our lives. So You expect more from us than from our relatives, friends, and others of the world. Teach us to be more generous than we have been, until now. Let us give ourselves totally, especially in those areas of our lives, where we have been holding back from You.

Luke 12:39-48

October 25

Jesus, when we hear Your words that You
have come to cast fire on the earth, we feel our
own hearts aflame. We know what You mean.
There isn't any time to be worried and
concerned about anything in the world, except
doing the will of the Father in heaven. That
must be our meat and our drink; it must be the
very breath of our lives — all we desire, think
of, and dream about. Give us that Spirit, that
we will desire to turn the world upside down, to
bring all people into Your keeping. Give us the
grace to begin with ourselves.

Luke 12:49-53

October 26

Jesus, when we look at the signs of our times, we realize that the end of this world as we know it could come at any moment. There are wars and rumors of wars, there is violence in the hearts of people all over the world, there is darkness and evil even in places that used to be sacred. Help us to be concerned, not only for ourselves, but for all others. Let our contact with all people be one of peace-giving, be a call to them to love You more, be a word of comfort to tell them not to be afraid, but to trust in You. Let us be instruments of Your peace, until the end.

Luke 12:54-59

October 27

Jesus, You reflect for us the Father's
compassion and patience. We have seen in
Your life on earth, how You always gave
another chance to those who failed in serving
You and loving the Father. We praise You and
thank You for this, but we ask further for
ourselves, and for all sinners in the world, that
You continue to give them another chance. Let
us continue to plead for their salvation through
the way we live, abstain from sin, love our
neighbor, and detach ourselves from all
worldly things.

Luke 12:1-9

October 28

F ather, we know that there is no power on earth that can do anything, without Your permitting it. We can see in Scripture, how all things worked together for Your glory and the accomplishment of Your will. We see You save the young Moses' life and let him escape his persecutors. We know that You are just as active in our own lives. So many times we have acted contrary to what you expected and desired of us, but you managed to teach us and lead us, even through the errors and sins we must claim as our own. We thank You and ask You always to keep hold of our hearts, that we will respond to Your touch, to Your call.

Exodus 2:1-15

October 29

Father, keep us always in the presence of the burning bush — the fire of Your creative love. We hear Your voice calling us, reminding us to remove our shoes — this is holy ground, when we stand in Your presence. The burning bush sends sparks of love into the world, the gentle breeze carries them in every direction. We are meant to be those who go to all places, spreading the fire of Your love. Lift us out of the darkness in which we often dwell; cut us loose from those attachments that keep us from burning in the places, where You call us; help us to follow You everywhere, for everywhere You are is holy ground. Thank You for these graces of Your call.

Exodus 3:1-6, 9-12

October 30

F ather, we see in the instructions that You
gave to Moses, that Your will is always
accomplished. But it is often delayed, and at
times we are confused by thinking that Your
will cannot be done. Remind us often of who
You are: Your name is, *I am,* which means
everything. You are *all*: there is nothing that
exists apart from You. Your name is the key
that can unlock the hearts of all peoples; Your
name is a light to reveal Your Spirit to all
whose eyes are opened. Your name grasps
every part of our being and reveals to us our
own secret name, which has been given us by
You. We call upon Your name at this moment,
to fill our hearts with the courage to be with
You, the strength and grace to follow You, and
to respond to Your call to us.

Exodus 3:11-20

Father, You gave Your people in Egypt the ritual of the Passover, which they would keep for all generations. The Blood of the Lamb was spread on the doorposts of their dwelling places; it was the door through which they would go to their freedom. It is the same doorway through which we find our freedom, also: the Blood of the Lamb. The depth of the mystery is too great for us, but we know somewhere deep in our hearts that without the blood of Christ, we could not be saved. Help us to be faithful to this Blood, to let it wash us free of our sins, to let it be the sign in which we live and breathe and have our being. We thank You, Father, for the Lamb of God.

Exodus 11:10-12, 14

November 1

F ather, we praise You, for all the saints who have gone before us and who have left such sweet memories of their lives in books and the communities they lived in. We realize that there are countless numbers who are not listed in our book of saints, but who are enjoying eternal life with You. We unite ourselves with every prayer they said, with every word of love they offered to You and to others. We hold up their lives to You, as we would hold a torch to light our own way and the paths of others. We sing their praises for the ages to come. We ask You to lead us, too, in the path they walked.

Mark 10:17-21

November 2

F ather in heaven, we give You praise for all
of those lives which were dedicated to serving
You. We realize that they, as we, were sinners
on their pilgrim way to eternal life, and also
had moments and times of failure and fault. We
pray that You would strengthen us, who strive
to follow in the way of Jesus, that we will end
our lives full of zeal and dedication to the
Gospel life.

John 6:37-40

November 3

F ather, You tell us that the Israelites had
been in Egypt for 430 years. Much of that time
they were in slavery; they waited a long time
for You to send their liberator, Moses. They
again waited a long time until You sent the
Messiah. And now we wait again for a long
time, until the world is changed into those who
love and serve You. It may take centuries yet,
before You gather all people into Your
Kingdom. But we can wait and trust and not
despair. Help us to work for that Kingdom by
our own lives, by getting rid of all darkness that
may be in us or around us. Help us to live for
that Kingdom, by always radiating in our lives
the spirit of hope, joy, and patience.

Exodus 12:37-42

November 4

S ometimes we are like the Israelites in the
desert. Father, we seem never to be satisfied
with all of the gifts You have given us. You
have given us so much that sometimes we are
fearful that You will expect much more from
us, more than You expect from those who have
little or nothing. Let us offer all we have back
to You, by sharing it with those who have need
of what we have. Let us carry in our hearts for
the rest of our lives, the image of those who are
poor in material things, spiritual things. Let us
have nothing, so we can have all things from
You.

Exodus 16:1-5, 9-15

November 5

The Acts of the Apostles tell us that the crippled beggar at the temple gate gave Peter and John his whole attention. Father, I'm begging something from You every day, and many times during the day, in the name of Your Son Jesus. But I seldom give You my whole attention; part of me is often somewhere else. I've given my energy to some other thing; my body is resting, my mind is wandering, my heart is filled with a hundred worries and distractions. Forgive me. Take my attention. Teach me to fix my whole self on You, when I pray.

Acts 3:1-10

November 6

F ather, we thank You for the insight that
You give us into Your will for us, when You
show us the commandments You have given to
Your people This is what You will and desire
for us, what we will and desire, as Your
creatures. Each commandment is a way of
loving, and a way of reaching You. We thank
You more for the gift of Yourself in Your Son,
Jesus. He came to show us how to go beyond
these commandments, in loving and serving
You. Help us to be open and sensitive to the
teachings of Jesus, so we will become all that
You created us to be.

Exodus 20:1-17

November 7

Jesus, thank You for showing us the way to be servants of others. You not only attended to the needs of others who were lacking or suffering in some way, but You lay down Your life for all of us, so we could have eternal life. You call us to do the same, for all others who have some need of us. We must give something of ourselves every day, we must give ourselves away — especially to those who are lonely, poor, or rejected. Help us, Jesus, to see the opportunities that are around us. Help us to be the servants of others.

Luke 22:24-29

November 8

Jesus, we are called to conversion every day
of our life; we are called to call others to
conversion, for as long as we live. Our first task
is with ourselves. It is easy to slip into faults
that tend to grow and even overwhelm us. We
can ignore them, we can be blind to our own
sins, we can become too lazy to reform and
truly get rid of the faults we have. Teach us,
Jesus, to be converted to You, day by day.
Help us to realize the joy that You have, when
You know that we are seriously trying to
reform, to get rid of our sins, and be totally
converted to Your way of loving and living.

Luke 15:1-10

November 9

Jesus, one of the joyful scenes in the Gospel is that occasion of Your entering the house of Zacchaeus. What an overwhelming experience it was for him! How Your light filled his house and warmed his heart! In an instant, his life had changed; he became a generous person, giving of himself to others. Jesus, I beg You to touch me, too, as You did Zacchaeus, so that I can pour myself out for others. Take from me that selfishness that has led me to seek myself in all things. Let me share with You the joy of giving to others in every way.

Luke 19:1-10

November 10

Jesus, one of the confusions of this life is that
we can become satisfied with the material
things around us. We can become so filled with
these things and the desire for them, that we
forget how passing they are, how all things are
destined to become dust. Open our eyes, our
hearts, so that we can gradually and daily let
go of all possessions. Even little things in our
lives can become too important to us. Open our
hands, so we don't hold on to anything; open
our lives, so we will be anxious only for Your
love and Your presence to us.

Luke 16:9-15

November 11

F ather, we marvel that Your chosen people responded so long ago to the covenant You made with them. Though they often failed, though many did not recognize Your Son Jesus, as the Messiah You had promised, they still have been faithful to the covenant. We pray for those today who are keeping Your Sabbath, that through our prayers and example, they may come to know Jesus for who He is, the Son of God. We pray and believe that before the end of time, all the people of Israel, all of Your chosen people, will recognize Jesus. Help us always to pray with faith and love for these whom You called to Yourself so many ages ago.

Exodus 24:3-8

Jesus, again we ask You to increase our faith.
There are times when we have no doubts, when
we can trust You and Your life for us in
everything. But there are also times, when we
feel cold and far away from You — when
everything that happens to us and to the world,
and to those we love, seems to tell us that You
have no care for us. Help our faith; help us to
be firm in our trust in You. Let us be unafraid
in the darkness, and persevering in our
following You.

Luke 17:1-6

November 13

Jesus, we haven't always been the kind of
faithful servants You want us to be. It was long
ago for most of us, when we promised to do all
things for the honor and glory of the Father.
But we have often been distracted, diverted, or
have done our work fitfully. Thank You, for
Your patience with us. We ask You now to
renew us in our vocations as Your servants; we
ask to be given again the enthusiasm we began
with; we ask that what we don't give, or
hesitate to give, that You take from us. We
truly desire for You to use us as You wish.

Luke 17:7-10

November 14

Jesus, thank You for reminding us of how
precious we are, in the eyes of our Father in
heaven. Sometimes we feel bad about
ourselves; sometimes we can't stand ourselves,
when we think of all the sins we have
committed and the petty things we have done.
But then we're reminded of the Father's love, of
Your dying to show us the Father's love, and
we feel good again; we feel like trying harder to
do the Father's will, rather than our own all the
time. Help us never to forget how we are loved
— how the Father loves us just the way we are,
with all of our weaknesses and all of our sins.
Thank You, for Your goodness.

Matthew 10:28-33

November 15

Jesus, You told us many times that the
Kingdom is in our midst, that it is within us.
We thank You for Your presence here, for
where You are, there is the Kingdom. You are
within us. We long for the day, when we can
have nothing else to do but to contemplate
Your presence within us, within everyone
around us, within this world. Of course, that is
only a dream, for once we can enter wholly into
the Kingdom, we will be able to think of
nothing else. Our whole being will be filled
with the love of being with You, in You, and
living through You.

Luke 17:20-25

November 16

Lord, we realize that someday the world is going to end. All of the beautiful things of Your creation are going to return to dust, to nothing. No one knows when that will be, and we realize that there is no reason to worry about it. If we live every day in Your presence; if our whole purpose in living is to do Your will and spread the Kingdom, then we have nothing to fear from the world ending, no matter how it may come about. We ask You for the grace and the energy to preach Your Word by our lives and example, so all people will be ready for and long for Your Second Coming into the world.

Luke 17:26-37

November 17

J esus, throughout history people have always
looked for God's coming into the world. Most
ancient peoples saw it as a great, earth-
shattering event, and even the Evangelists
pictured Your birth as announced by angels,
shepherds, and visiting kings. But Your
continued presence in the world has been
missed by most of Your creatures. We haven't
looked for You in prisons, the slums, among
the despised populations of the world. We
haven't always seen You in the poor and
starving, the weeping, and those screaming in
desperation. If we don't recognize You where
You have said You are, how can we know You
when You come at the end of our lives?

Matthew 25:31-40

November 18

Lord, we remember how Moses' face shone
after he had come from Your presence. It was
as though the light of his spirit, of his whole
personality, of the image in which he was
created, shone in his face. We believe that the
closer we come to You, the more we will be
transfigured. We pray that day by day You will
lead us in our prayer, and in our love for one
another, closer to Your presence. We know
and believe that without Your willing it, this
cannot be done. But we know also that we have
to keep ourselves open to Your leading us —
sometimes through suffering and pain,
sometimes through periods of darkness and
dryness. We must ever hope and keep praying
that You will transform us to become like You,
in as many ways as You permit.

Exodus 34:29-35

J esus, You have taught us that we can't be Your followers; we can't even know You, unless we turn away from all things. That doesn't mean, we realize, that we are to have nothing to do with other people or with the world. We are called to preach Your Gospel of love by our work, our lives, our example. But You are telling us that we cannot love other things more than we love You; we cannot cling to any possessions that would keep us from loving You with all of our hearts, souls, and minds. At this moment, we renounce and turn away from all things that may stand between You and us. Thank You for Your inspiration and Your calling us to a life of love.

Luke 14:25-35

November 20

Jesus, You come to me in so many ways, each day of my life. I wish I could be like Zacchaeus each time You appear; I would throw open the doors of my house, I would rush out to welcome You, I would give my attention to You fully and completely. I would love having You with me.

I am sorry that I'm not always conscious of Your coming to me in the thousand ways You do during the day. I pray for the grace to be more aware of Your being here, of Your being in those I meet, in Your being in the things I do all day. Deep in my heart, I really want to be more loving.

Luke 19:1-10

Jesus, someday we hope to see the whole history of creation, from the beginning until the end. We hope to understand how all things that have happened and will happen work together for good, for Your honor and glory, for the salvation of human beings. We have such a narrow vision as humans, that we can see only the here and now; we can't see tomorrow, let alone Your Second Coming. But we do believe that You are present here now. We believe that, if we hold onto the knowledge of Your presence and Your love, then we will be ready for anything that happens. Increase our faith, renew our hope, give us love.

Luke 19:11-28

November 22

Jesus, we thank You for this day, and for the love that people in our country shared with one another today. But we think of those who had no one to love them, of those who had nothing to eat. We know the day will come, when You will sit in judgment over those who have it all and have not shared with others. We pray for Your grace, so that we will never forget the poor and hungry, that we will always share ourselves and all that we have with You, in the person of all those, hungry, naked, in prison, sick, or in any kind of need.

Luke 19:41-44

November 23

Jesus, we who have been baptized into Your
body have truly become temples of God. You
have blessed us by Your presence in us, so that
we have become sacred places. We believe that
in some mysterious way You dwell in us, that
we can pray always in Your presence, as we
enter into our own silent spirits.
Teach us how to pray
    by entering into the depths of ourselves;
teach us to recognize Your holy presence
    in all those who believe in You;
teach us to recognize all the world
    as a sacred place, where Your Spirit is
        always breathing love and life.

Luke 19:45-48

ather, let us never doubt the power You have over all of creation. We read how You shared this power through Your various prophets, through Moses, as he lead Your people out of Egypt. Remind us of how You have used Your power in our own lives: You have often led us out of darkness, out of the control of Satan; You have taught us to come to You in all of our needs. But especially the power of Your love has drawn us to You, day after day in our prayer, in our patience to bear ills, in our trust that You love us and will take care of us. We thank You with all of our heart, for letting us recognize You as our Lord and our God, our God and our all.

Exodus 14:21-15a

November 25

F ather, we thank You for the way in which
You have led us through the desert of our lives.
Sometimes we have been in a dark cloud that
seemed to last for years, but You finally led us
in the light of the journey. We know and
believe that we must always trust You, no
matter how impossible everything seems.
Where else could we go, except to You, to find
our way into the eternal life Your promised?
Though we grumble at times, as Your chosen
people grumbled in the desert, we want the
grace to trust You and put our lives entirely
into Your hands. Thank You for giving us the
grace to ask for all we need, to stay close to
You.

Exodus 40:16-21, 34-38

November 26

J esus, teach us what it means to deny our
very selves. We know that we must let go of all
material things in this world, of anything that
would keep us from possessing You. We ask
You to enter into the depths of ourselves, so
that we can see and understand how we must
let go of the life we cling to, how we must
abandon everything into Your hands, that we
must somehow embrace nothingness, in order
to have You. Teach us, Jesus, to deny
ourselves day by day, so that at Your coming,
we will have no hesitation in leaving all things
in this life, to be with You for all eternity.

Matthew 16:24-27

J esus, the only way we can let Your light shine before the world, in the darkness, is if we have Your light within us. There are often times when we don't know what to say or what to do. But if we look into our hearts and say or do what You tell us there, then others will see Your presence and respond to You. But we need to renew Your presence every day by our prayers, by our reading Scripture, so we will feel at home in Your life and try to identify with everything You did and said, while You were on earth. Jesus, remind us each evening to look back over the day and examine the ways in which we could have done better, and rejoice at those times when Your presence was obvious.

Matthew 5:13-16

Jesus, there seems to have been times in the history of the church, when there were ample laborers for the harvest. Orders and communities multiplied; there were plenty of workers for humanitarian and social needs. Today our resources are limited and getting smaller in some areas. Jesus, we pray to the Harvest-Master and to You to send the laborers that are needed, so Your Gospel can be known. We pray that we will recognize them, when You send them. We realize that they need not fit our idea of a disciple, but only Your idea. Help us to recognize the new patterns of ministry and the new kinds of ministers that You will send into the world.

Luke 10:1-9

November 29

F ather, we are used to reading of the miraculous things You did in the history of the people of God. Through Your messengers, Your angels, Your prophets, and Your Son, You caused great and amazing things to be done. Open our eyes to see the miracles that You accomplish in our lives, day by day. The greatest miracle that is always before our eyes is the miracle of life — our own, and that of all Your creatures. Everything our senses can respond to is in existence, because You have brought it out of nothing. How beautiful life is! How beautiful all creation! We praise You and thank You for all things. Teach us and help us to recognize the holiness of all things. Help us to move reverently through our time on earth and especially praise You for all other human beings in whom You live.

Genesis 17:1, 9-10, 15-22

November 30

Jesus, we thank You for Peter's brother Andrew, whose feast we celebrate today. He responded, as did Your other faithful disciples, to Your invitation to abandon all things and follow You. After Your resurrection, he carried Your words to other lands and gave his life in witness to You. It was long ago that he chose to walk in that way, but even in our day his life and work is still fresh. Those words that he began are still going on somewhere in the world, and his example still inspires Your church on earth, as it will to the end of time. Thank You, for Andrew and for all the apostles, who gave their lives for You.

Mark 4:18-22

December 1

Jesus, it could happen to any of us that we become involved in the things of the world for our own sakes, just for the pleasure of achievement and work; we could forget entirely that, as Your disciples, we are supposed to work to establish the Kingdom in the world. Help us to keep from giving ourselves to the wrong things, for the wrong reasons. Let us search our hearts in Your presence, so You can show us where we are inclined to err, and what we must do to give our energy, talents, and love solely to bring You honor and glory, and not for any other purpose in this world.

Luke 21:34-36

December 2

Jesus, I know that You are still ignored and crucified in our day, by people who claim to follow You but never think of You, by people who mis-interpret Your teaching and pervert it, by those who praise You with their rules and rituals but whose hearts are far from You. Forgive all of us. Help us to be awake, to be renewed, to be filled with Your Spirit so that our love and acceptance of You may show in our love of one another, and especially in the way we welcome all people in Your name, and await Your coming.

Acts 4:1-12

December 3

Jesus, thank You for telling us through
Matthew, that faith is not limited to one place,
one tribe, or culture on the earth. In the long
history of the preaching of the Gospel, we have
seen how people of all the world have
responded in faith to Your Word and Your
Spirit. We ask that there will be a continued
conversion of all countries and cultures, that
our own country will be renewed in faith, and
that all who live here will show a Christian
concern for the poor and needy. We pray that
all will seek first the Kingdom of heaven, and
that the thirst for peace and tranquility will
motivate all elected officials and all who care
for Your truth.

Matthew 8:5-11

December 4

Jesus, unless we would have the experience of having no faith at all, we cannot fully realize how blessed we are to have been given the chance to know You, to believe in You, and to love You above all things. Help us to share that faith with others, by helping all whom we live with, work with, and associate with, to deepen their faith. Our good example and our prayers can do that. Let us offer prayer and sacrifice for all those in the world who haven't had the chance to know You at all. We want never to cease praying for those, so that through the efforts of those who believe, they, too, will come to the faith. Thank You, Jesus, for this grace.

Luke 10:21-24

December 5

Jesus, because You were so fully human,
You know firsthand what it was to be hungry,
what it was to suffer physically and to see those
whom You loved suffering in the same way.
Your heart was so full of compassion that You
felt compelled to touch them and heal them, to
work a miracle to feed them. Now that You
still live on this earth, in all those who believe
in You, give encouragement to them to do, as
You did — to seek out the poor and hungry,
the sick and suffering, and to take care of their
needs. As long as You are hungry and suffering
in anyone, all of us have the responsibility to do
something about it. Give us the insight; give us
the courage.

Matthew 15:29-37

December 6

Jesus, we pray Your forgiveness for having
neglected to respond to Your Word. We have
heard You speaking to us for years; Your
words have poured upon us as a daily shower of
rain. We have been soaked in it, and yet the
result of our response is meager indeed. There
is little we can show, as the result of our labors,
for all these years. We remember You saying
that "Unless the Lord build the house, they
labor in vain who built it." Help us build more
substantially the work that You have given us
to do. Give us the strength to try harder and
the will to persevere. Let us give all we are, in
response to the word You speak in us and to us.

Matthew 7:21, 24-27

December 7

J esus, there have been times in our lives,
when we didn't realize how blind we were. We
didn't see how unloving we were toward others;
we didn't see how unforgiving we have been to
others; we didn't see how all of our time and
efforts were directed to our own good. But now
we realize how much we still need Your help,
to know what to do to change our lives. We
need to see now how You want to lead us to do
the Father's will in all things, by loving others
more humbly, by loving ourselves less selfishly.
Give us the faith to know and to understand.
The faith to see!

Matthew 9:27-31

December 8

We praise You, Father, for the great love You
have shown for the human race, which You
created in Your own image and likeness. We
thank You, Father, for Mary, a consummate
example of what You desire all human beings
to become. We thank You for making this
possible through the humanity of Jesus,
through His giving of Himself so totally for us.
We ask You for the grace to concentrate so
thoroughly on the example of her obedience
that we will set our wills to do likewise. We
glorify You and thank You, Father, for her.

Luke 1:26-38

Jesus, we have read that the apostles were joyful that they were judged by the Father worthy to suffer for the name of Jesus. There would be more suffering for them and for the whole Christian community. But even these afflictions seemed to draw more people to following the Way: the blood of the martyrs was the seed of the church. Let us remember that about our own disappointments, trials, or suffering. We know they can be valuable in Your sight, if we bear them in the right spirit — patiently, even joyfully carrying them in Your name. Thank You for that grace.

Acts 5:34-42

Jesus, as we read the story of Your healing of
the paralytic, we are reminded that sin can lay
us low, that it can truly paralyze us and keep
us from doing what we are called to do, from
becoming what we are called to become. Heal
us and forgive us, that we might be free. We
didn't realize that years of being unloving,
years of being selfish, can make it nearly
impossible for us to do anything that is good.
Everything we do is marred and scarred by our
own paralysis. We must be released from this,
or we shall never be what You have called us to
be. We beg You now to touch us; forgive us all
our sin, cleanse us whiter than snow with Your
holy, precious Blood, and let us walk to You,
free and healed.

Luke 5:17-26

December 11

Father, we give You thanks for the plan that Jesus revealed to us: that it is not Your intention for any of the lost sheep to be truly and forever lost. We realize that anyone can choose to be lost. But we know that in Your mercy, You intend for even these to be saved. So, during these days of Advent, we offer You our most heartfelt prayer for all of those who are not now looking upon Your face and desiring to be with You. We pray for anyone who finds sin more attractive than You. We would like to offer our whole lives for these sheep. We implore You, we beg You to touch their hearts, so they will turn completely to You. We thank You for hearing our prayer.

Matthew 18:12-14

December 12

Jesus, we know that You always spoke what was in Your heart, but those words, calling to Yourself all who are weary and who find life burdensome, are most precious to us. We can see into Your loving heart. In our hearts, we know that You died for each one of us individually, as well as collectively. The only response, then, can be to Your love; the only response You desire is our love. From the very depths of our hearts, we offer it to You. We offer our whole selves. We let go of anything else in the world that we are clinging to; everything else fades away except the love we have for You. Purify it and claim it as Your own.

Matthew 11:28-30

Jesus, You tell us that it is the violent who capture the Kingdom of God. We know that it takes a complete commitment to You and Your teaching, in order to enter into the Kingdom. We have seen it in the lives of the saints, from John the Baptizer to the martyrs of the present day. When people who believe in You and love You, give themselves in martyrdom, they are taking the final step in the same journey they have been walking for most of their lives. Help us to walk that way each day: to show our commitment in our thinking, our acting, our living and loving. Let us be totally Yours, no matter what the cost.

Matthew 11:11-15

December 14

Father, we like to take time, now and then,
to thank You for some of the brilliant lights
You caused to shine in this world. We are
grateful to You, for the life of St. John of the
Cross. We know of his suffering, his study of
scripture, his preaching and writing, but most
of all his prayer that has been an inspiration for
so many people in his own time and through
the centuries. We thank You for him, because
the warmth of his love is felt in our own lives.
Just by reading the words of his burning heart,
we are led to praise You more, to be more
serious about our prayer, to long more ardently
to be with You. Give us the gift of longing for
the day when we shall be present totally with
You, and in the company of all Your saints.

Matthew 11:16-19

December 15

Jesus, we thank You for John the Baptizer.
Whenever we hear his name, our thoughts are
filled with the memory of his courage, his
complete dedication in announcing Your
coming as the Messiah. Many prophets
preceded him, announcing the days when You
would appear, but John was the greatest of
them all, pointing to the past and to the future.
Let us hear his voice and respond to his call:
to look for Your coming every day of our lives,
to find You in the sharing of the Eucharist,
to discover You in all our relationships,
to offer You all of our sufferings and work,
to live in Your presence
    with patient trust and perseverance.
Jesus, let us always thank You for St. John and
give You praise by our imitation of him.

Matthew 17:10-13

December 16

Jesus, we know that the early church grew rapidly in numbers. People from all ranks of life were called to follow in the Way, and all who began to live in Your name, lived to serve one another. There was none among them who wanted to seek honor for himself, but all wanted to be of service to others. Whatever work we have to do in life is meant to be done for the good of others. One job is not more important than another. Every work is meant to give us an opportunity to pour out love, so that others can be blessed and God praised. We, like Christ, are meant to bring God's love into the world by our serving others. Help us to understand this and practice it.

Acts 6:1-7

J esus, we thank You for the gift of life. We thank You for all of our ancestors who have handed on to us much of what we are. We are especially grateful to those of our relatives who have shared with us the gift of faith, who have encouraged our growth in faith by their own example and their prayers. We ask You to let us continue to pass on this gift, in our relationships with everyone we know and meet. Fill our lives so that our words and example will be cause for others to draw more closely to You. We know that it is only through Your generosity that we have believed in You, and it is only through Your love of us that we can share in spreading the Kingdom of God.

Matthew 1:1-17

December 18

F ather, we thank You for the example of
Saint Joseph, who responded to the word he
received in a vision or dream. Though others
may have told him he was going against the
rules, he accepted Your word, trusting that
You would provide for what would happen.
We ask You for that grace, too, that we will be
open to hearing Your word, wherever it may
be spoken to us. You still speak to us in
dreams. You speak to us through others,
through books, and the events in our lives. We
need a sensitivity to the work of the Spirit, to
know what You are saying to us and when You
are truly speaking. We want to trust
completely that You will guide us in our
response to You.

Matthew 1:18-24

F ather, today we pray for all of Your chosen
people of God, throughout the world, as they
celebrate the feast of Hanukkah, the feast of
lights. We know that they are commemorating
the dedication of Solomon's temple, so many
ages ago. We pray that they will give You the
honor and praise that is due to You, the Most
High, and that their worship will always be
pleasing to You. We pray for those who are
suffering persecution anywhere in the world,
and we hope that their patient acceptance of
the rejection they suffer from others, will be
cause for the salvation of their persecutors. We
ask for Your grace, so we will show them the
love You expect us to give them.

Luke 1:5-25

December 20

Father, we can only marvel at the
extraordinary way in which You have entered
into the history of Your human creatures. You
sent Your message to an unknown maid in an
insignificant place with the intention of
sanctifying the world, all of creation, and
bringing it into Your heavenly Kingdom.
Truly, we know that Your ways are not our
ways, and Your thoughts are not our thoughts.
Help us to rejoice in these events we celebrate
at this time of year. Help us above all to give
You the kind of honor and glory You expect
from us, the kind of praise we owe You, our
Creator, the total love You expect from us.
Thank You, for the help You give us to do
that.

Luke 1:26-38

B lessed is she who trusted that the Lord's words to her would be fulfilled." Lord, Elizabeth spoke those words which have been on our lips from our younger days. We have been taught to appreciate especially the loving trust that Mary had in Your words to her. Her trust in You was total, not only at the beginning of Your work in her, but all through her life with Jesus, and into eternity. We thank You for that gift of trust You gave her. We ask that You let us share in that trust also; help us to be open to all You want of us, and all You do in our lives. We want to place our entire selves into Your hands, and we ask You to do with us as You will.

Luke 1:39-45

December 22

F ather, we give You thanks and praise for
the Magnificat of Mary. It is a song of praise
which we would like to be an essential part of
our own lives. We recognize our own
nothingness and unworthiness, and we praise
You for blessing us so tremendously, in spite of
it. We thank You, for all of the good things
You have promised the poor and lowly. We
thank You, for sending Your Son Jesus to the
poor, with the promise that they shall inherit
the Kingdom of heaven. We ask You for the
continued grace to respond to Your call, and
will let go of and reject all things of this world.
We ask You to let us share in the lowliness of
Mary.

Luke 1:46-56

December 23

M ary, we realize that Your heart was united
with the heart of Your Son, from the beginning
of His life on earth. We believe that, as He
lived out His life — with all its frustrations and
worry, its suffering and grief — You were
united with Him, suffering with Him, grieving
with Him.

Lord, help us to be more faithful to the
example of Your Mother. Unite our hearts like
hers, with Your heart. Teach us, through her
example, to be generous in our love, to bear our
burdens with patience and even with joy. Help
us to trust that, through all of the darkness of
this world, You will lead us into the light of
God's love.

Luke 2:1-9

December 24

Father, Your servant Zachariah foretold the coming of Your Son, to lead all people out of darkness into the eternal light. As we celebrate the anniversary of His birth, we pray that we may continue to carry that light into the darkness of the world, where we live. You have given us the gift of faith in Your Son Jesus, and through that gift, we are given the light to guide us in the way we should walk, the way we should live, and the way we should love. Pour out Your Spirit upon us; send Your Spirit into all of the world, that all people will know and love You and serve You in the teachings of Jesus, Your Son.

Luke 1:67-79

December 25

J esus, we are without breath, as we
contemplate Your coming into the world. You
came in a strange place, a poor place;
You came helpless and defenseless.
We can't help but think on this, Your birth
day, of Your dying day, so helpless, so empty
of anything to call Your own, in such a strange
and lonely place.
Help us to finish the days of our pilgrimage,
walking with Your Spirit, in a world where we
are strangers.
  Help us to live among the poor
    and rejoice in being poor.
  Help us to let go of everything
    that may make us forget You
      and why You came to this earth.

Luke 2:1-14

December 26

F ather, when Stephen was stoned by the angry crowds, he prayed for those who killed him. He realized that their hatred and ignorance had deprived them of all reason. And he could still love them and pray for their salvation. Give me a desire for everyone in the world to come into Your Kingdom. Especially, let me pray and hope for the salvation of those whom I have not loved as You have called me to do. Change my heart, that I may pray sincerely for all those I have a hard time loving. I pray for all people to come to a knowledge and love of You, especially the self-righteous and self-satisfied.

Acts 7:51—8:1

Jesus, we remember how one of Your chosen ones, St. Paul, began as a persecutor of the church, of those who loved You and believed in You. But You changed him around. Perhaps it was through the prayers of those he persecuted, that his life was changed. I pray You give me a greater confidence that You do heed our prayers — especially those which are offered for the spiritual growth and salvation of others. You once said that You would pray for Your apostle Peter, that Satan would not control him. So let my prayers for others keep them from evil and lead all of them to eternal life.

Acts 8:1-8

Jesus, we know that many of Your early followers gave their lives in witness to the truth of Your teaching. They were filled with Your Spirit and feared nothing in this world. They believed that You had captured their whole being and nothing could separate them from You. Help us now to live that truth. We have given ourselves to You by our own choice. We belong only to You; You are our life. We know and believe that You will never leave us. Help us to be faithful in what we have chosen to do and be. Help us always to be converted in the most radical ways.

Acts 6:8-15

Mary, you belong to Saturdays,
   to the day before Christ rose from the dead,
   to the day before your Son was born.
You belong to the early morning,
   to the light before the sun,
   to the yellow and orange and pure white rays
      of sun, leaping up from the horizon
      through the blue, filmy clouds.

You belong to my Saturday morning,
   to the dew on the grass and awakening
      flowers,
   to my awakening heart;
   to my morning at the sacrifice of the Mass.

Mary, you are my Saturday,
as I walk through the day,
And as the day ends, and the sun rests.
I see you go before me,
promising me a resurrection in your Son.
I long for that day when I will be with your Son
                  forever.

Mark 11:27-33

F ather, we thank You and praise You for the great love You have for all of Your creatures, and for the great love You offer freely to all people. We know that You call everyone to believe in Jesus, Your Son, and in You, who sent Him to this earth. We know that You offer Your Holy Spirit, to all who open themselves to You. We thank You for the faith You gave to St. Peter, who recognized the working of Your Spirit in the Gentiles. Increase our faith, so it will influence others to love You more, and deepen our own response to the Holy Spirit. Teach us to consider other, new ways that we can bring the faith to others. Each generation challenges us in different ways. Help us to respond according to Your will.

Acts 11:1-18

December 31

Jesus, we know that in the early days of the church, the Christians continued to worship in the Temple and in the synagogues. They were accepted in many places as faithful people, but in time they were rejected and not listened to by many of the Jewish elders. They were persecuted and driven from the places of worship. We recognize one lesson from this: There is always darkness to be overcome, if Your Word is to be heard and seen and believed. Even in our own days, in our own communities, in our own lives, we have to overcome resistance to Your Spirit. Pour out Your Spirit upon us, so that whatever You will for us and for others will be done, that we will help bring Your light with each new year.

Acts 13:13-25

NOTES